# *HI! MY NAME IS MIKE!*

## I ONCE WAS LOST

# Michael A. Luciani

**BOOKMARK**
COMMUNICATIONS

*Hi! My Name is Mike*

Bookmark Communications LLC

Norman, OK 73069

Rights Department, Norman, OK 73069

Manufactured in the United States of America

10 9 8 7 6 5 4 3 2 1

Library of Congress Cataloging-in-Publication Data is available.

ISBN: ISBN: 978-0-9996507-3-8

# Contents

# Foreword

As you read my story, it is my prayer that you and your family will find hope, courage, strength, and mercy through the power of the Holy Spirit and Jesus, the Son of God. It is my hope that no matter what this life throws at you, you will be overcomers through the good, bad, and sad times. My prayer is that you will enjoy my journey and learn from it as you read.

Thank you and God bless!

Michael A. Luciani

Jeremiah 1:5
*I knew you before I formed you in your mother's womb,*
*Before you were born I set you apart and appointed you as my*
*prophet to the nations.*

On June 30, 1962 at 4:26 a.m. I was born to Bernie and Mary Luciani on a hot summer day in Pittsfield, Massachusetts. (That's what mom told me anyway!) I would be #2 out of 4 siblings. Linda was born in 1961, me in 1962, Beth in 1963, and Daniel in 1966.

Dad and Mom were hard-working, blue-collar folks. They were middle class and kept their same jobs for almost 40 years. Me, I was Grandpa Luciani's favorite, and I never knew my Grandma Nancy Luciani since she passed away before I was born. Families aren't supposed to have a favorite, but maybe that's why I was named after Gramps. He could grow one of the biggest vegetable and vineyard grape gardens you would have ever seen! Man, he had a green thumb!

All of the aunt and uncles and the rest of the family would get together on Friday and Sunday evenings to pitch pennies in card games with watered down orange soda and vodka, drinking Miller Beer, and some were smoking Lucky Strikes. At 10 years old I would love a sip or two off of anything Gramps or anybody was drinking, some even liked the Cold Duck wine. Aunt Gloria would always make the Apian Way pizza and baked cheese toast on rye bread.

While the adults were playing cards, all of us kids would be in the living room playing board games and watching TV. If I didn't get my way with anything the way I thought fit, I would raise a ruckus and get a butt whooping at least 4 times a month when I got home. I guess you would call it the strong-willed child syndrome.

I remember summer of 1972, I was just 10 years old and there was a small, wooded area where my friends and I would build tree forts. On this one particular day, I was alone and here comes Walter walking up. Walter was a character, and not only the town drunk but a midget. I started making fun of him and cussing, so he started cussing back at me. So, I started throwing pretzels at him. He started throwing rocks at me and he said, "I'm going to tell on you." I said, "Uh-oh!" and jumped missing the branch and falling about 7-8 feet to the ground. He saw it and was laughing at me. I went home crying and ended up in the hospital with a broken right wrist, and I had bitten my bottom lip. Walter and I became good friends after that. Talk about learning respect for my elders. Come on! Mayberry RFD, had Otis, for some of you old folks. LOL!

As I was getting older, I never dreamed of the road I would take. I always wanted my way or the highway between the ages of 7-12. I lived in a small town, had a cool family, was a churchgoer, and a Catholic altar boy for 5 years.

My church would always have a picnic for us at Mountain Park every summer in Holyoke, Massachusetts. The best part out of it all was spending time at Fenway Park from 1971-1979. I remember my first Red Sox game my dad took me around my 9th birthday. I was freaked out when I saw the green wall out in left field, The Green Monster! The Sox would win 4-3. Sonny Siebert pitched and we beat the Brewers.

The family would go to 2-3 games a season after that, to see the Boston Red Sox. What a time to be a Red Sox fan! The hope and anticipation of winning a world series was unbelievable until the curse of the Bambino (Babe Ruth) was finally broken in 2004. But as I was getting older, I was getting burned out on the scene. I could never make the local little league team, which I always felt it was political. The coaches always seemed to pick the kids that lived on their street that could hardly play. That was my opinion anyway.

But my last year of eligibility, my friend Jay's father would sponsor a team called Monteleone Floor Covering. That year we were all the misfits of an expansion team and we went 0-18. I remember it like yesterday.

The game we could have won was against the best team in the league, BIG N. A ground ball to shortstop, throw to me at first out. I threw the ball to home the catcher dropped the ball and we lost. HA!

The next few years would be junior high school, grades 7-9. At this point, trying to find my way with other kids would be challenging and we never ruled out anything. So then and there, I decided to start my rebellious streak. Even though church was still there, I would start to steal the wine that the priest would drink and hoard Three Musketeers candy bars at the rectory. Man, those nuns were a trip! But I fooled them all with my, kill-them-with-kindness routine. Well, at least I thought I did!

We had so many good times with the family during the junior high years from 1974-1977. But, just as life happens, the ones around you who you love, will certainly die at some point. We had July 4th picnics and birthday parties. I played baseball in summer and basketball in the winter. Grandpa Luciani was a stickler for getting all his children and grandchildren together. I think he felt more comfortable with the family around.

My other grandparents were also a blessing. We would always go over to Grandma and Grandpa Gallagher's house during the week, and a lot on Sunday afternoons too. But during the week, I would walk home from Crosby Junior High School and stop to see them around supper time. Grandma would make the most killer goulash!

I would sometimes sit there and listen to Red Sox games on the radio with Grandpa Gallagher alone. I would sneak a couple of swigs of his Pabst Blue Ribbon which would be nice and cold. I would also hang out in the bedroom with my great aunts, Bess and Nan. My Uncle Sonny and I would ump little league games a couple of years later. Doubleheaders were a blast! In between games, he would go to Jimmy's Bar and Grill for a couple of beers while I went to the top of Clapp Park and smoked a couple of doobies to get good and ready for game 2.

In September of 1977, I would start high school. It was kind of freaky for me not knowing what to expect. I met more friends than I could imagine that got high on a regular basis. Things went kind of okay. I took autobody vocational classes: one week of shop and then one week of classroom studies. As 1978 came around, Grandpa Luciani's health started getting bad. I saw him a few times that year, but between adolescence and not knowing or caring about death, it was only about me. I got on the school bus to come home on Nov.7th, 1978, and I think my sister told me Grandpa had passed away. Inside I felt a little cold and numb but didn't know what to think or say. I went to the funeral and didn't cry, the family always said that's what made me spin, but personally I thought it was the bag of weed and the half pint of Yukon Jack in my back pocket.

Along came 1979, and my sister's boyfriend bought a Polaris TXL snowmobile around 8:30 in the morning. By high noon, I had totaled it. I hit a tree with no helmet on, full throttle. If I flew headfirst into the tree, I would have been dead. I broke my left wrist, lacerated my right knee, and was down and out for winter break. I was still on crutches when I went back to school. I started healing as spring came around, and I started really liking girls. I found one I liked, and her name was Donna. I needed cash, so I would work a little shoveling snow and mowing lawns, but as soon as I earned it, I spent it on Led Zeppelin, Kiss, and Cheap Trick: Live at Budokan albums and drugs.

I remember Auntie Nan's closet had a shoebox full of cash, so I would take a $10 or $20 here and there just to get my weed money. See, when you're a drug addict, you don't care how you get your fix or who you hurt. They got hip really quick and I think they started blaming Uncle Sonny, but that's what I heard through the grapevine. So, I stopped stealing. Right around then I told my mom on June 30, my birthday, "I'm 16 now. Two more years, and I'm out of here!" She said, "That's right! Go get a job!" She told me, "I want $25.00 a week. I cook your meals, do your laundry, and you have a bedroom. I want $100.00 a month."

That was horrible I thought, so she got me a job at the Friendly's Ice Cream Restaurant where she worked washing dishes. The only thing I thought about was free food and stealing cash out of the tip boxes. Sometimes I would hit the lady workers' purses for a ten spot here and there, just to fill my drug addiction. That job didn't last long, but I rode it out as long as I could.

I met a friend named Paul through a good friend, Larry. He was about 10 years older than me, but he had and could get the goods. I started selling pounds of weed and hash, but when you get high on your own supply that doesn't last. I came home one day and my mom was standing at the kitchen door with a black trash bag full of my stuff: a pound of weed, scales, bongs, rolling papers, and a big pipe made out of surgical supplies out of the operating rooms used for surgeries. She said, "Get rid of it!"

I still needed a job, so I begged and pleaded with my dad to get me on at the hospital with housekeeping. Well, he got me on a graveyard shift and I had to work weekends. I think maybe they thought it would make the party scene dwindle, but it got only worse. My first night on the job, a co-worker named Kearn O'heara, told me if I was feeling tired, I should go into the employees' lounge and take a nap. Boy, was I gullible! He went and told on me. Busted! However, we did become good friends later. Half of the night crew were potheads, so we would sneak down to the operating rooms and take the doctors' surgical clothes. Man, were they comfortable! The best time we had was turning on the nitrous oxide tanks and breathing it in. Boy, what a high! I remember I was so high, I leaned against a table that had wheels on it. It took off and crashed into all kinds of equipment. I started getting burned out on this job.

A couple of weeks after Kearn O'Hara and I became friends, he asked me if I wanted to go see REO Speedwagon and 707 at the Springfield Civic Center in Springfield, MA.

I told him, "Give me an hour to find out if I can go." I called him back to say, "Yes, let's go," and he told me he sold the tickets. He told me to come anyway because I could probably buy a ticket from a scalper.

So, we drove to Springfield and as they were going into the concert, I couldn't find a ticket. Scalpers wanted anywhere from $60.00 to $100.00 a ticket and I only had $40.00.

As I was walking around the area, this guy walked up and said, "Do you want to see the concert?"

I said, "Yeah, how much?"

He said, "$20.00."

I said, "Give me the ticket," and he said, "No, give me the money and follow me."

So, we walked a half block behind the Civic Center, and he walked me up to these glass doors. The door opened and he handed a cop the $20.00. He led me to the elevator and up to the second-floor walkway behind the stage. My friends found me 10 minutes later because of the Ted Nugent hat I was wearing. Therefore, I got into a concert for $20.00. What a blast!

Around this time, all my friends were at the Stateline Bar drinking and listening to the local band, Crazy Annie. The band was named after a bag lady that hung around North Street which was another popular hang out on Tuesdays and Thursdays. What a nightlife in Pittsfield!

One Friday night I decided to go to the Stateline. I started drinking sloe gin fizzes, along with popping some black beauty pills and yellow jacket pills until I was buzzed. It was now 10:00 p.m. and I had to be at work in an hour. Well, I didn't show up until about 12:30 a.m. and the boss man was off of work, but his little sidekick, I called Yimmer, was waiting for me. He wanted to wear the daddy pants so bad!

I came in the locker room to get ready for work, he said, "Where you been?" I was buzzed out of my mind and I told him, "None of your business, little Yimmer."

"I'm going to tell on you!" he said. I jumped up while he was in an office chair and I kicked him in the chest. Over he went! He got up and told security on me. One of the security guards was the dad of a good friend of mine. He came and said, "Luciani, you're drunk?" and slapped me in the face. I said some nasty things and to make a sad story short, that was the end of my house-keeping career at Berkshire Medical Center.

The only thing sad about this was that my friend, Harold, had the same hour job as mine, and the same payday every Thursday. We would cash our checks, buy weed, and go to the grocery store and cook up a bunch of frozen food munchies at my mom and dad's house. We would get tired, walk home, and I would sleep for 12 hours. Now we would not be able to do this anymore.

I met Harold in elementary school. He sat behind me and we had those old wooden flip top desks. I would always open his desk and it was called Chachi's Junk Desk. It was full of hostess snacks and all kinds of junk wrappers and sandwiches.

1979 was ending and I was looking forward to 1980, my last year of high school. I had a girlfriend named Donna, I was head over heels for her, probably because I was always getting high, and drinking beer, and hav-ing sex with her. I was a mess and thought I never had to play by the rules and had no accountability to anyone.

My best friend, Larry, had gotten his license, so his parents gave him a Vista Cruiser station wagon. We had a blast, drinking and partying and smoking weed all over Pittsfield. We would cruise over the mountain to New York State, buy a pitcher or two of Genesis Beer, get hammered, and drive back after shooting a couple of games of darts. You see, the drinking age in New York state at the time was 18 years of age, and we would get served without any ID. Pitchers were $2.50, and the minimum wage was $2.65 an hour.

Well believe it or not, dad talked to a Mr. Tanner at Sunoco gas station. They were looking for someone to pump gas and check oil. I got the job by walking across the street to the gas station and talking to him. I would start to steal cases of oil to help with my so-called happy sacks. (weed)

One day the boss man fell and broke his ankle. He had a bottle of painkillers. I asked him for a couple, and he said, "Take as many as you want." I ate three and within 20 minutes, I puked so bad I left work and slept for about a day and a half. I went back to work like nothing ever happened.

Things were going pretty good, so Larry and I took a weekend trip down to Cape Cod, Massachusetts in 1980 to see Rush in concert after they released the album Permanent Waves. We had to go see them! We got the tickets, got on The Cape, parked, and we just took a cab to find the motel. I don't even remember if we had reservations or not, but I do remember pulling out a pint of Yukon Jack in the front of the cab where I was sitting and asking the cab driver if he wanted a sip. Larry had busted up laughing, but the cab driver said, "No, too early for me." It was about 10:00 a.m. so I took a swig and put it back in my carry bag.

We got to the motel and the manager gave us a key. We got to our room and there was no T.V. To top it off, within less than an hour since we had been there, the concert was canceled. Neil Peart, the drummer, had broken his wrist. We tripped! So, the best thing we could do was fill up the bathtub with ice and a case of beer and we started getting buzzed. I went to the office and asked the manager for a T.V., and he gave us one, but by the end of Saturday night we were so bored and restless we started raising hell and being loud. I remember Larry opening the motel door and the manager was out leaning against a fence with his arms and legs crossed, just staring at us with an evil glare. So, we slammed the door and turned off the lights and started talking smack that we better be quiet. We did and he went away.

We got up the next morning and headed back to Pittsfield. I remember one incident of my mom coming up to the school while I was in the shop that week. She was mad and I found out why. As she was walking up the stairs going to my bedroom, she looked at the perfect angle and as she turned her head, she could see a Seagram's bottle of whiskey under my bed with a couple of shot glasses. The only reason she was going to kill me was that it was a Christmas gift she had stashed that was wrapped all nice, and I opened it. But she later cooled off after talking to Mr. Diamond, who was assistant principal. I always seemed to have favor with this guy and I never knew why.

Mr. Diamond, the vocational director, and my counselor called me in for a meeting. They said, "If you just show up everyday for the next two months and bring a pencil, we will pass you."

I kept my end of the deal!

I was having the 'not-give-a-darn' attitude about nothing. I had about 2 months to go until high school graduation and I was not doing well at all. My home life was falling apart, and I was not getting along with mom. I did not want to do anything. I thought Donna and I were okay, but physical and verbal abuse was setting in. All I wanted to do is get high and have sex. Thank God I did not get her pregnant! We went to the prom but had a bad time. I thought she loved me, but we spent the night together both miserable. She went home, and things were a-changing.

A couple of weeks went by after the prom, graduation was getting near and I was still working pumping gas. I did not see too much of my friends because of the work schedule. The morning of graduation, I threw on a pair of Levi's and my Mork and Mindy T-shirt. I ran up to the school, sat in my seat, and heard all the speeches. Mr. Diamond asked us all nicely not to throw our caps. I got in line, received my diploma, went back to sit in my seat. Before he dismissed us, we all threw our caps in the air.

Well, I achieved it. I got my diploma and I thought to myself, "Who cares?" But as my journey continued in life, that little piece of paper would land me many jobs over the years, so deep in my heart I did do something right for a change.

I kept working, partying, and seeing Donna very little. My friends and I would hang out and occasionally go to Pam Plunkett's house, which was our flophouse get high, drink, and rock out. Her parents were so cool, and she lived in a nice rich area also. She was always a good friend of mine.

Less than a week after graduation I finally had a day off. It was Sunday evening, June 22nd, 1980. I gave Theron a call late at night and asked him, "What are you doing tomorrow, Goody?" (That was his nickname.) I told him I had Tuesday off, which was the next day. He said, "Yes, let's get together!"

Well, I woke up early and went to his house around 9:30 a.m. We had a blast and played whiffle ball, threw the football around, smoked weed, and went to lunch. Later in the afternoon, we rode motorcycles through the woods and then we went back to his house and chilled out. I think we watched a movie and listened to music. I was just with him all day.

Well, it became late as we were walking towards my house. We were passing Angelina's Sub Shop and I said to him, "Let's get a sub."

He said, "Cool." We had meatball subs and kicked back there on the picnic tables. It was around 11:30 and I told him, "It's getting late. Got to go since I have to work tomorrow."

He said, "Cool, I'll see you tomorrow." I said, "Okay, 'night," then I went east, and he went west, both of us heading home. And I would never see him again.

Morning came and I talked to Larry. I told him I had to work until 7:00 p.m. and asked him to pick me up after work. He said, "Okay," but he was always notorious for blowing me out because he was seeing Sharon and new friends were coming into the cocaine circuit.

Anyway, I was working, and I saw his car drive by the intersection of Center St. and West St. around 6:00-6:15. He usually never came by and I could tell he was going to party with other friends, so I said, "Phooey!" Around 6:40, just 20 minutes before quitting time, I heard the gas pump bell ring and I looked over. It was Marylou Martin and Barb Staubach. They were cool friends. (I used to call them Harvey and Roger because of Harvey Martin and Roger Staubach, because I was an avid Dallas Cowboy fan back then and those guys were players.)

Anyway, they yelled to me, "What time are you getting off, "Lucie?" I told them in twenty minutes. They asked me if I wanted to get high, and I said, "Yes, but Larry is supposed to come to pick me up."

Well, they came back I locked up the station. Larry never showed up, so the girls and I drove down to Clapp Park and started throwing a frisbee and smoking weed. I looked up and here came Kathy and Joe who were really good friends. We all got high and it was getting dark and late. For some reason, I told everybody, "See ya," or maybe they left before me.

Anyway, I walked home feeling tired and I put the TV on and hit the HBO box. That's when it was just a button and a key you turned on. I put on the movie Grease and just laid on the couch. The telephone rang and I answered it saying, "Hello?" The voice on the other line was frantic and he said, "Is Mike home?"

I said, "This is mike." He said, "No, Mike is dead."

I said, "Who is this?"

"This is Chucky Carlo. Mike is dead."

I said, "Chucky, this is Mike."

He again said, "No, Mike is dead! There has been a terrible accident and Mike is dead."

Larry has been in a terrible accident and two people are dead.

I told him again, "Chucky, this is mike. I'm ok."

He said, "Okay," and then hung up.

By this time, it had woken mom and dad up. We were puzzled. So, dad and I went to the hospital, and there was Larry's dad sitting all alone. He was in a fog, kind of dazed and confused. My dad bought him a pack of cigarettes and we asked him what was going on. He did not know much. All of a sudden, my Uncle Bob walked in. He was a Pittsfield Police officer, and he was standing there with two DMV officers.

He said, "Michael, I saw that car and I was looking for you, but I didn't see you." Me, being Mr. Wiseguy, I said, "Nope, not this time."

I asked to see Theron's body and they said no, they would not let me. Dr. Wasser came out and asked me if I would like to see his son, David. I said, "Yes," and he brought me back to the emergency room. There I saw David hanging there with wires and hoses. I never asked, but now I look back at it, David was in so much trauma. He could not lay down. (Please remember this scene.) The so-called High School Graduation of 1980, which took place on June 18th, 1980, had us all torn up less than 5 days later.

I remember going to Theron's home where all of us met. His mom, Vicky, came to the door and I just remember hugging her, as she said, "Michael!" All us kids were trying to cope with it. Young men and woman crying and condoling. One of the girls said something and Vicky started yelling. I guess that was her way of venting.

To top it all off, within a month, my high school sweetheart broke up with me. We tried getting back together a few times, but I was angry and hurt. I didn't even want to talk to her. So, I just went back to hanging out with my pothead buddies down on Worthington St.

I remember sitting in my room one night at end of the summer of 1980 listening to REO Speedwagon's Hi Infidelity 33 1/3 LP album, and hurting over everything I was going through. I was thinking about killing myself, but I didn't have the guts. I looked over near my pillow, and there was an ounce of weed, so I started smoking and getting high. I didn't care, but all of a sudden I said, "The heck with this! I'm gonna kill her!" (It was just trash talk.)

I continued to work, but as 1980 ended, 1981 came I was in no man's land. Larry ended up going to court, and the parents of the deceased, Theron and Bobby, wanted Larry to pay dearly. He ended up doing 90 days in the county jail.

February 1981 came I was jobless and homeless for a while, staying on my drug dealer's couch. I also stayed with a good friend of mine him and his wife. They decided to have a keg party with Heineken, and I got smashed. I walked down the stairs during the snowstorm, and I thought no one saw me. I went right to the snowbank, but Sharon did and followed me. They got me back upstairs and I was drowning in my sorrows and crying about how much I still loved Donna. I was so drunk!

Mom and I made up, so I went home for a while. A couple of months went by and I found out Joe, who I was with that night at Clapp Park, was also supposed to be in that car, but his girlfriend Kathy was adamant he hadn't been spending time with her. Thank God he spent time with her that night. I finally caught up with Larry and Joe they were talking about going to visit Joe's aunt and uncle out in Southern California, in Monrovia. I asked them to let me go, but they said it was only going to be a two-week vacation.

I said, "That's cool." I was 18, I had about $850.00 and I had a little saved and my tax return had just come. I remember that the round-trip ticket was about $500.00. Well, April 1981 arrived and all 3 of us jumped on a plane and headed to southern California.

We were picked up at the airport by Uncle Jack, Aunt Kitty, Cousin Kathy. We all went back to Monrovia and relaxed, then they brought us to this place called the Steer Burger. I always remember that place because the cheeseburgers were huge along with Olympia Beer.

That two weeks flew by, and I was hinting that I wanted to stay for about the last several days and I did end up staying. Larry and Joe went back after two weeks I ended up staying ten years!

So, here is where my California experience started: Please buckle your seat belts! Some of you may think, "Yeah right," but remember, all of us have a story to tell.

Romans 6:23-
*For the wages of SIN is DEATH, but the gift of God is eternal life in CHRIST JESUS our LORD.*

There, I started meeting some of Kitty's friends through the American Legion. I met a man named Bill who ran a mattress warehouse. At first, I thought, "Yeah, this is great," but as time rolled by, I could not stand him. He was just another drunken guy that would take advantage of things. Don't get me wrong, at first, I was so appreciative of things.

I started driving and delivering mattresses around Arcadia, the Pasadena area, and then most of southern California. Heck, I started learning the product so well, I became a pretty good salesman. Or so I thought.

Bill had a wife named Marylou and we got along so well. She was cool, but at times I thought she was fed up with her husband's drunken stupor and horse gambling. Remember, Santa Anita Racetrack was less than two miles away from job, and the bookies would always show up. I didn't know anybody at the time, and every Sunday the L.A. Times would have this concert section. When I opened it up, there was a pic of Ted Nugent staring at me. I just had to go to the SCREAM DREAM TOUR.

So, I took a bus to downtown L.A. by myself. These four dudes opened up their first American show in lavender jumpsuits. I found out later it was the band U2. I was sitting around getting high smoking weed with people I didn't know, but as the concert drew to a close something told me to leave, so I did. The Holy Spirit was even with me then and I didn't know it. As I got close to Arcadia around midnight, I remember the bus driver telling me the last two buses I took were the last ones of the night.

I kept on working, writing to so-called friends back home, and one even sent me a ¼ gram of cocaine. I remember Kathy laughing at me while I snorted away. I used to go to the park and play basketball with people I would meet. They were all potheads. I thought I had it made.

As a few weeks rolled by Kitty's husband, Jack, was not feeling well. He had surgery and as the Drs. opened him up, he would pass less than two weeks later. Well, things were not going well between Kitty and me, and it was time to move on.

Inside the mattress warehouse was a ceramic store owned by sweet people. All of a sudden, they told me they had a garage apartment in El Monte. I knew it was Kitty and Bill working behind the scenes to help me. I jumped on it for $ 225.00 a month-not bad! I had no transportation, but the company would let me drive the mattress truck home.

I stuck out like a sore thumb! KLOS 95.5 was the rock radio station and they always had oval shape bumper stickers of bands they would give away and I plastered the black bumper with them. One day I was driving home on a side street, I saw this guy on a beach cruiser bicycle wearing a nice white shirt and black pants and he flagged me down. Frank was his name, and we became good friends. Found out later he was working at Von's grocery store as a stocker. I started meeting all kinds of druggies to drug dealers. I would have all kinds of parties at that little house.

I remember loading up the box, that's what we called the mattress truck, with about 10 of us to go to the Forum downtown L.A. to see Van Halen. I think it was a 1984 tour. Anyway, we were out in the parking lot drinking beers, smoking weed, and taking hits of acid. By the time I got in the arena I was wasted out of my mind. I remember trying to push the bouncer to the side and he was fighting me not to reach the stage area. I wanted to get upfront so bad! I kept yelling out his badge name: Bob.

"Come on, Bob! Let me upfront! Please, Bob, please!"

He finally asked me, "Why are you calling me Bob?" I said, "That's your name badge."

He said, "NO! I'm badge # 808!" LOL! I was a mess! Concert ended and I drove home. Another mercy trip that I made it home safely.

A few weeks later, I was driving to work in Buena Park on my Honda CRM 450 motorcycle. It just so happened it was a day I wore my helmet. As I got off interstate 5 on Beach Blvd., I headed south and drove upon a construction site. As the traffic was flowing, a Ford Pinto stopped, and I bounced off the rear end of it.

As I lay there in dismay, full of pain, a police officer walked up and looked down at me. He said, "Good boy. You wore your brain bucket." So that was another time that God was looking out for me. I went to the hospital and ended up with just bangs and bruises.

This was about the same time that Richard Ramirez, the so-called "Night Stalker Killer," was haunting southern California. Out of fear and because he had killed someone not far from where I lived, I went and put $50 down on a 357 Magnum. I never ended up picking it up because of all the drugs I was on.

We would constantly have parties at that little back garage house. I would meet some of my neighbors and we would have Whiffle ball games. It was just a nice, quiet neighborhood until I showed up, but I was very respectful to anybody until you would make me mad, LOL!

I felt like I was 6"4' and bulletproof. What did you expect? I was 18 years old! Anyway, as time went by, I was working, partying, and going to concerts. I was working in the back of the warehouse unloading a truck when this girl walked by. I said, "What's up?"

She said, "Nothing."

I asked her name and she said it was Candy.

I said, "Cool." We became good friends and she told me, "You have to meet my twin brother, Randy.

I said, "Cool." I met him and he just started playing guitar, and he was good! After a month or two, he asked me to get a bass guitar.

I said, "No, it's cool. I don't even know how to play it."

He said, "Come on, I'll teach you."

I said, "Nah."

At that same time, my landlord's son was going to church at the Calvary Baptist in West Covina, CA. He asked me if I would join the softball team. I said, "Sure."

Well when I showed up, I just figured out I was in the middle of Jesus freaks! Pray before the game, pray after the game. I never would. I would show up with a California Angel's helmet on plastered with heavy metal stickers on it from Iron Maiden, Judas Priest, and Black Sabbath.

Well finally last game of the season, the team pastor was adamant that I pray, so I did, but it meant nothing to me at the time. Little did I realize the Lord was having them plant faith seed into my life.

My heathen lifestyle continued. Frank had shown me a picture of his sister Andrea in her high school parade outfit, and I asked to him who it was. He said it was his sister, Andrea.

I told him, "I'm going to nail her!"

He said, "No way! She's not like that!"

Within a year and a half, she was pregnant. I continued to work, and her parents hated me. At the same time, I had bought a bass guitar, Ampeg amp 8x10 inch speakers, and an SVT TUBE HEAD. Between work and going back and forth to practice with Randy, things were not going good with Andrea, but in April of 1986 on the 22nd, Brittani would be born. WHAT A BLESS-ING! I LOVE THAT LITTLE GIRL!

At first, I thought things were working out, I would get up in the morning with Britt, place her on rocking chair as I prepared her bottle, and feed her while we watched cartoons. But after a couple months, it was not working because Andrea and I did not get along, never mind loving each other.

Time would go by and she would bring a guy friend over she went to school with. He was an El Monte police officer. I think they tried to scare me. I went, "Boo," but did nothing stupid because, in the past, my relationship with Andrea turned violent a couple times.

## JOHN 8:36-
### *IF THE SON SHALL MAKE YOU FREE,*
### *YOU SHALL BE FREE INDEED.*

We were arguing one day and she told me she was leaving.

I said, "Bye, I'm going to see the Scorpions tonight in L.A."

Well, to my surprise when I got home the condo was gutted and she took everything, including my daughter, but not my rig. I still had my bass, amp, and stack of speakers. The next day, the owner of the condo came over told me to get out. She showed me straws, razor blades, and cocaine residue.

She said, "Get out or I'm calling the police!"

So I loaded up my stuff and went to Randy's house. Frank and I would still be in contact. I even remember crying out to God, only for a moment, but I would always remember the Lord's prayer that my mom made me learn growing up in Catechism. I had no idea at that time God was listening.

I told Randy, "We need to practice."

And I was terrible, but as time would go by, we were getting better. Randy's mom was looking to buy a house in Bloomington, CA, out towards San Bernardino. I was living in Ontario, CA, about 45 minutes west of Bloomington.

GALATIANS 6:7-
*BE NOT DECEIVED GOD IS NOT MOCKED,*
*FOR WHATSOEVER A MAN SOWETH THAT*
*SHALL HE ALSO REAP.*

I was working in Rancho Cucamonga at the time, so that's why I was living in Ontario. I was trying to balance the band and work in mattress warehouse sales, but I would bring my little cassette stereo. Iron Maiden just came out with Somewhere in Time. And that's the way I lived my life. I would work in that small warehouse, smoke weed, drink Michelob Light, and snort hefty lines of coke while waiting on customers. I was so polluted.

A customer gave me $20.00 cash for a bed frame, and I put it in my pocket. Well, the driver saw this and went and told on me. I stepped out to get some party balloons for a birthday party that evening, I think it was for Randy's girlfriend, when I returned the owner was there and fired me on the spot. Little did I know my insides were shot. (That was my spirit man talking to me.)

Well, we went out to dinner and I went home and got high and drunk. I woke up the next morning shocked. I had no job, so I contacted a friend of mine and he fronted me a couple pounds of weed. That kept me afloat for a couple of months. I went and found a job driving a parts truck into downtown L.A. It was a culture shock: $9.00 an hour starting pay. I was making from anywhere from $500 to $800 a week depending on sales at the mattress warehouse.

Would it have been different if I wasn't so high on drugs and alcohol? Maybe, but the enemy had me so bound and gagged, and I did not know anything about spiritual warfare then. I just continued to be beaten up and do things my way.

I would go back and forth between Bloomington and El Monte. Frank had just rented an apartment hitched onto this house that these Brazilian people owned. At the same time, Randy had met this brother duo from Chicago. They had just moved to the area. Paul and Chris. Paul would become our lead singer, and Chris our roadie crew.

About the first month, it was just some big old party. We would play, party, hardly play, party, but they were good guys. We were still in the process of trying other singers also. One day, around the corner from our studio was our friend, Mick's, house. He was a drummer and he had a friend named Darren who was trying out to be our singer. Well, Darren had a girlfriend named Becki, whose mom was Darlene. (Do you see where this is going?)

Darlene asked Becki, "Who is that?" I was carrying my bass guitar.

Becki said, "That's Mike."

Darlene told her, "Tell him I think he is cute."

So that night I drove up to the motel where she was staying, but it was black as can be-no lights on. I think she passed out and went to bed on some blackberry brandy she was drinking. LOL!

But it was not the beginning of the end. We would finally hook up. I came to her apartment a few days later and brought the wine coolers, and she had the meth. We ended up staying in bed for 3 days partying. The ups and downs would define our relationship for three years. I would go back and forth between the band, Blooming-ton, and El Monte. Darlene would finally settle up in Phelan, CA, a small desert town up near Victorville, CA. I would come and go.

One Friday night was different than any other. The band was going nowhere, Randy wanted to party, Paul and Chris were over with Randy's new girlfriend, Pen-ny, and I told them I was going up to Phelan to be with Darlene. They were calling me all sorts of names.

I told them, "Heck you! I'm going to get some!"

Well, Saturday went by, no biggie. Then Sunday went by, then about 4:00 in the morning Monday, our band manager Lance knocked on the door of the trailer.

I said, "What the heck what are you doing here, and how did you find me?"

He told me he remembered the school bus garage across from the trailer where we were staying. Then he began to tell me that there had been an accident and Randy had been in it with Paul and Chris.

I told him to chill out here until morning. We smoked a couple of joints, slept an hour or two, and when we woke up, Darlene made us breakfast. Then, down the Cajun pass on I-15 we went. We met up with Randy's mom and sister,' Candy. We were told that both brothers were killed. Whoever was driving hit a utility pole on Foothill Blvd. in Rialto, CA. We were still finding tools half a mile away from the impact of where the car hit. (Remember David Wasser earlier in the Pittsfield accident?) They took us to the emergency room and there was Randy suspended in mid-air with tubes and wires.

God was not getting my full attention still. I would meet up with Paul and Chris' family, the dad, grandma, sister, they were all in shock dismayed. And what do I do? Hand them a case of Genesee Beer. They were beer drinkers, so I guess that was the only way I knew to console them. I went to the funeral and ironic as it could be that they passed away on April 1st,1990.

Ezekiel 28:13-15-

*Thou has been in EDEN the garden of God, every precious stone was thy covering, the SARDIUS, TOPAZ, and the DIAMOND, the BERYL. the ONYX, and the JASPER, the SAPPHIRE, the EMERALD, and the CARBUNCLE, and GOLD: the workmanship of the tabrets and of thy pipes was prepared in thee in the day that thou wast created. Thou art the cherub that covereth; and I have set thee so: thou wast upon the HOLY MOUNTAIN of GOD; thou hast walked up and down in the midst of the stones of fire. Thou was perfect in thy ways from the day that thou was created, till INIQUITY was found in thee. (How beautiful LUCIFER was before his fall from heaven.)*

Randy was home within a month from the hospital. I went to visit him and we talked. He was scared out of his mind that everyone was out to get him, especially Paul and Chris' family, and the law. He kept on telling me, "We have to get this band in gear! The time is now."

I was so manipulated and lost. I just wanted to rock out, so I said, "Okay."

Well, Darlene and I started not getting along again, so I left. I was going back and forth between Bloomington and El Monte. I stayed with Frank a few times. He was working and started up his meth business while I was going back to Bloomington for band practice. We still needed a drummer and a singer.

Our small studio in Randy's garage was not cutting it, so we rented a music studio in Azusa, CA, which was between Bloomington and El Monte. Randy and I would show up to the studio, just me and him for about a month, playing and writing our demonic music. (That's why I put Ezekiel 28:13 in here.) Before lucifer's fall, it says THE WORKMANSHIP OF THY TABLETS, AND OF THY PIPES WAS PREPARED IN THEE IN THE DAY THOU WAST CREATED, YOU SEE HE WAS IN CHARGE of all the music in heaven, and look what happened when he fell, I always wondered why there was so much demonic music on the face of the earth????).

So, I started to hang out in El Monte again. I told Darlene she needed to go out with Bill, a geeter truck driver, but then again, we were all geeters at the time. LOL!

Frank lost his job and we needed to make money, so he started selling meth. Darlene was with Bill. I knew she hated it, but he was taking care of her and the kids. I was still missing Darlene. Meanwhile, Frank had called a pager company to come by the house. We called it HEMLOCK FRIKE. Hemlock was the street corner, and we took our initials between Frank and Mike and we made up HEMLOCK FRIKE. Any way this older gentleman came by to sell us pagers. We sat with this guy and talked a bit. Then the first thing out of the man's mouth was, "I know a lot of people who get these pagers like to sell things in small plastic clear baggies."

We said, "No, we need it strictly for communication."

A few months went by and I was missing Darlene. I was going back and forth between the studio and El Monte. Well, one day the studio owner came in and told us that he knew a drummer that liked to play the same time of music. His name was John. He came in, we played a couple of songs, and it clicked. He had a double kick bass drum set and it felt good to have drums because I was the bass player. We played a month and he asked if we needed another guitar player.

We said, "Sure."

He brought his friend, Kirbo, over and he could play those killer lead parts. Within a month, we had written songs, such as: Perish Priests, Grown to Matricide, K.T.B., Blunt Force Trauma, Eerie Calm, and Speedratic.

Sure enough, we needed a name for the group. Within two weeks, BRUTAL IMPACT was born, and I never really thought about it until now, but I think it was named after that accident Randy was in. We jammed, we played gigs, then we took more breaks.

I would find myself back in El monte and Bloomington, partying, rocking, but after a while, I began missing Darlene a bunch.

I told Frank, "Let's go up to the high desert. I don't feel right. We need to get out and have a break."

He kept on saying no, so finally one day I told him, "I'm going and you are more than welcome to come with me."

I would be watching Cubs-Giants playoffs in about 1989, dropping hits of acid, and talking to Darlene on the phone. I was on so many trips, I would never leave my house! I would have a Boston Red Sox plastic helmet on with my head in a small fridge and my feet near a wall heater. I was melting, at least my mind was fried on both ends of my body, because of the drugs.

A few weeks went by and I could not get Darlene off my mind. We hadn't talked for three months, so while watching the Broncos and Steelers, I decided to write her a letter. I found out that she had been calling Bill by my name. She later told me that she told God, "If he is supposed to be in my life, let me hear from him."

Well, a few days later I wrote her a letter and brought it by Darren's house and gave it to his brother Aaron.

Darren asked her, "Do you still love Mike?" and she said, "Yes."

Well, he gave her the letter and she called me immediately.

I finally told Frank, "I'm leaving, and you can come with me if you would like."

He said, "No."

The next morning, I stuck a 2-inch screw in my little Toyota through the carburetor, and off I went. I made it up to the high desert, but there was this one stretch of mountain road about 5 miles I had to make. Well I did, and it was about 10 miles an hour took 40 minutes, but the Lord was with me, even though I had no clue who He was!

Bill was living with Darlene, but he was a truck driver. I went when he was gone. One night he came home very suspicious. It happens to be when I was in the bathtub. She ran in the bedroom and Bill followed, seeing my luggage.

He yelled, "Is someone in there?!"

She said, "Yes, Mike."

At this time, I was standing dripping wet with a towel, and I grabbed an iron. I didn't know what to expect. I thought I was going to have to flatten him, but he just ended up leaving. I was still rocking out and trying to have things my way, but as time went by, within three weeks Frank's house was raided by EL Monte P.D and DEA, they were riding him hard.

"Where is your roommate? Tell where he is!"

Frank told them I had left weeks ago and had no clue where I was. At the same time, a co-worker of his walked up just to visit him and they thought he was me. His name was Mark. They said he was crying like he was peeling onions for a banquet of 400. LOL! They finally let him go. Frank ended up doing 90 days in L.A. County jail.

While I was at band practice, we started getting good and we were jamming every night. Finally, small gigs started popping up and we were getting connections. Randy was still living in fear, so guess what? We went up to the high desert to stay with Darlene, but that did not last. While Darlene's two boy, Paul and Gary, and I were playing whiffle ball, Darlene told me when she looked over at Randy before we left, she could see a demon through his eyes. By the next day, we had to leave, and she would not give me my bass guitar.

Randy and I drove to my bank and withdrew $50.00 and never looked back. We drove out to Malibu beach, where we slept on highway 101 on the coastline. Randy told me he had a brother that lived in Reseda, CA, and we could stay with him. (Well, we only stayed for two days.)

We drove back to Bloomington to his mom's house. As time went by, we were playing and working hard in the studio. Darlene would move back down to Fontana and move in with her mom. That's another demonic story in itself. I refuse to go there!

As weeks and a couple of months went by, Frank was released from jail. We met up and I finally invited him to the studio to watch us play. He loved it he thought we were a unique demonic hardcore thrash band. We were drinking, smoking pot, doing lines of meth, and all of a sudden, the door to the studio opened. It was a reggae band from the studio next door headbanging with us and they were tripping. When the night ended, we went our separate ways. I might have gone back to work because I had to eat. LOL!

2 Thessalonians 3:10 KJV-
*For even when we were with you, we commanded you this: If anyone is willing not to work, neither shall he eat.*

36

Darlene had moved down to her mom's house in Fontana and that would last only about 2 months. It was around Halloween 1990 that I was staying at Randy's house, but this one night I went to visit Darlene at her mom's house. We kicked back awhile and she let me watch the Rams and Steelers game.

It was around 11:00 p.m. so I decided to go back to Randy's house I didn't make it two miles when San Bernardino sheriffs would pull me over. Had no reason why they would, but when they checked the truck out they found a tire knocker (Billy club) and an empty bag of meth in the glove box. So, they took me into the county jail and booked me. I was coming down off meth, so I passed out and fell asleep for a few hours. When I woke up, it hit me like a ton of bricks. I asked this Mexican guy if I could read his Bible and he gave it to me.

I went through the book of Revelation in about a couple of hours, waiting for my name to be called to talk to the OR officer. They finally called my name, but I had to wait in the small cell area between the guard and general population.

As I was sitting there, I heard these footsteps, clicking heels really hard on the concrete floor. I looked up it was an inmate. He turned and looked at me and said," 'F' GOD!" Then he turned and walked away. Not less than two minutes later, they opened the cell door to visit with the OR officer. He asked me what I was in for.

He then looked at me and said, "You're a disgrace to the Italian people." He gave it to me.

After talking a while, he said he would try and release me. I went back to general population, got on the phone, and I finally got a hold of Darlene. She vouched for me, and I was released. We went to Burger King and munched, then she dropped me off at my truck. I went back to Randy's. I would finally pay fines and get charges dropped.

Darlene would move on to a hotel. I went by and to visit her a couple of times at the Premier Inn and gave her $200.00 so her and the boys had a place to stay a couple of weeks.

Things were starting to move rapidly with the band. We were finding gigs in Pomona, CA, and a place called Spanky's in Riverside California. We were opening up for bands named God Flesh and Napalm Death.

Darlene then found a place on Reed St. The Mexicans were rummaging through the empty apartments across the way, so she would come by Randy's mom's house and plead with me to come to stay with her. At times I would, but at times I wouldn't. Trina and Eleanor that lived next door would become friends with Darlene. Heck, they would go to Stater Brothers local grocery store and load up their baby carriage with steaks, roasts, and meat-expensive cuts. We ate pretty well for a while. I was not around one day, and this Mexican guy tried to give Darlene and the boys crap, so Trina beat him up. LOL! I remember Darlene had to spray back all the cockroaches. Man, her apartment was spotless, but the one next door was plastered with them.

I left for band practice and I was staying with Darlene on and off. I met the guys at the studio and we were playing and practicing hard for that Spanky's gig, but something inside me would NOT let go of Satan's grip totally. I remember John and I were working on a song called Erie Calm it had a beginning bass solo which John thought was cool, but as the band world turns, Randy did not like it because he didn't come up with it. Well, Kirbo, the other guitar player, liked it and majority rules, so we kept it.

I really did like John and Kirbo. They were cool guys and easy to get along with. Anyway, we played and practiced at all hours of the night for about a month. I was burned out from driving my box truck to downtown L.A. every day for an electrical supply warehouse, doing lines of meth to cope with life, and I was burning out fast.

I remember taking a couple of days off from work after I almost crashed and burned into a semi getting on the ramp of I-10 headed back to the warehouse. I came into Randy's house. I don't really remember the time or date, but it was a Monday afternoon and Candy, Randy's sister, and Doris, Randy's mom, told me to call

Andrea, Frank's sister, so I did. And when I did, my jaw dropped. Frank had been murdered. Shot straight in the forehead with a 357 magnum in El Monte.

1 Corinthians 15:55-57-
*O Death where is thy sting? O grave, where is thy victory?*

The sting of death is sin, and the strength of sin is the law but thanks be to God, which giveth us the victory, through our LORD JESUS CHRIST.

I remember going to Frank's funeral and seeing him lying in that casket. You could see where they put the putty filler and flesh color paint, but you could tell, it was horrible.

I started handing out flyers to our gig, and everybody was thinking just by looking at me: What a mess! Remember, I was in a death thrash band so of course it had to be cool, right???

I get out of there after telling Darlene that my good friend and my daughter's uncle had been murdered. Well, a few weeks went by and it was showtime. I remember driving down to Spanky's Café on Riverside. I went there alone because Darlene did not want to go. I pulled up and had a very heavy heart because I did not belong. I was thinking, "What the heck is going on?"

I did NOT know this then, but it was the HOLY SPIRIT convicting me. I went to the show straight to meet up with band members. They were dissing me, and I felt alienated. I also found out Randy started cheating with Kirbo's girlfriend, Melissa. When you're in a band, that is the #1 cause for break up and 99% of the time when bands fall apart.

-Well, Godflesh played, then we were up. Napalm Death canceled because their lead singer had a throat infection. We were jamming and having a great time, even though my heart was heavy. We had military for bouncers from March Airforce Base. They were super cool.

Well, remember that song Eerie Calm? It started out with my bass solo. We were jamming, then in the middle of the song the solo was to happen again, and I totally missed it. Brain freeze! Thank God for John, the drummer, because he nailed the cymbals to cover for me.

Soon our set was done, and everybody came up to me for high fives, both bouncers and people in the audience. They were saying how great of a job I did.

I said, "Thanks," even though I blew it. And there you have it, my 5 minutes of fame. We were packing up our gear and I still felt so isolated from everybody. I took my bass and went home to Darlene.

About the same time, Darlene met this girlfriend named Terry. Terry's mom ran apartment buildings on Juniper St, still in Fontana. I called Randy told him I needed to pick up my SVT AMPEG 300-WATT HEAD and my 8x10 inch speaker box, that so I could practice. I never looked back and have not been in contact with any of them in over 20 years, accept our band manager, Lance. We have been best friends and he has even come out a couple times to visit me in Oklahoma.

Anyway, Darlene and I were looking to get out of the Reed St. roach-infested hell hole. We finally moved in there on Juniper St., and it was such a blessing. Darlene's family was still down on me, but who cared as long as I had my weed and meth? I still didn't have a care in the world. Things were going pretty well for us that year. As a matter of fact, it was the best Christmas we ever had thanks for the drug money I made. Darlene's youngest son, Gary, was playing little league baseball, and I remember one game when I was geetered (methed out of my brain.) He hit a base hit with a man on second in the bottom of the 7th to win it 1-0. It was a very proud moment!

Times were changing fast. I still had my bass equipment, so I ran an ad and sold my 300-watt head only for $350. Gary walked home from school one day and asked, "Where is your truck?"

We ran down to the carport to see what he was talking about and it was there. We were confused, but about the same time, the apartment manager's son was getting out of prison to come live with the manager. Darlene's nephew moved in across the way, selling drugs also. One day my friend was coming over to give me a couple of pounds of weed to sell, but right next door a small house was being raided with men in hazmat suits and they were walking around the backfield of the apartment also. We were scared! I was calling my drug dealer to tell him not to come by, but when the dust settled, they were not after me.

The drug dealer came by anyway, and that deal was complete. Darlene's nephew at the same time brought a birthday package wrapped up for his daughter. We put it in the closet, and he never came and got it. A few days later Darlene had a bad feeling about that package. She opened it, and it was over a pound of weed. She called her nephew to come to get it. It felt like we were being set up, and God was telling us to stop, but we still played awhile. Really, her nephew's house was hot, and he was afraid of being raided, so he brought it to our house. He wasn't trying to set us up.

Well, folks around the apartment complex were telling us that their apartments were being broken in with no forced entry, Darlene and I put 2 and 2 together. It was the manager's son that had just gotten out of prison. He was getting all the keys to the complex. So before it could happen to us, we changed the locks on our doors. The apartment manager found out and was very upset.

Remember, that part when Gary came home and said my truck was gone? Well, this time it was the manager's son stole it. We filed a police report, and they found it down the street a couple days later. We were still being watched and arguing with the manager of the apartments for changing locks. We would have lost everything if he had broken in, and when I say everything, it was all about losing our drugs. LOL!

MARK 8:36-

*For what shall it profit a man, if he shall gain the whole world, and lose his own soul?*

Anyway, Darlene's middle daughter, Darlene, (we call her Sis) had called and wanted to come to visit for a while. We said sure and at the same time, Darlene kept seeing this ad in the paper for a church in Redlands, California named Hosanna Christian Fellowship. I couldn't stand her daughter. Super-Christian, but I guess it was a good thing. She saw my weed habit and told me I was going to hell for sinning. I blew smoke in her face.

She and her mom decided to go check out that church. They went a few times, but I kept saying, "NO, NOT GOING!"

Darlene came back and said the pastor called her out of the seats and started prophesying over her about her past hurts, and he said he saw a headboard with bookcase compartments with a burgundy Bible that had not been open in a while. He saw some other nick-knacks in the compartment of the headboard. I started laughing because one of the knick-knacks was a grim reaper bong that I used to take hits out of the back of its head and the pipe part was in its lap.

Darlene kept telling me, "You need to come to check this church out."

I said, "No way."

A couple of weeks went by, and she said it was really good, God was dealing with me to go, so I told all of them I would. One Sunday, as they were getting ready to go to church, I said I would go. I told them to get in the car and I would meet them downstairs in the parking lot. I went to the bathroom really quick and snorted a line of meth about 8 inches long.

I said, "Okay, let's go to church."

I felt this weird feeling and thought it was the drugs, but it was the HOLY GHOST ANOINTING! Please take my advice: Never go to church on meth (geetered.) HAHA!

I guess things felt pretty good the following week. They wanted to go back, so I said I would. This time though, I smoked a joint before we left. It sure felt a whole lot mellower.

I think I took a couple of weeks off after that. I remember when I first walked up to that storefront church, I could feel the anointing of God. That glory cloud was so thick, it was like such a thick fog that you needed to cut through it with a knife. Was it the drugs? LOL, I don't think so.

So, Paul, my stepson decided to go on a Sunday night. Things inside me were feeling so much different. We were at the church and LaMarco, head of music, was playing piano and singing and the Spirit of God fell. While LaMarco was playing, the Holy Spirit was telling folks to come up to the altar, and that somebody out there needed the Lord. Well, everybody that was in their seats ran up there except me. I started crouching down trying to hide behind the seats.

Finally, LaMarco said, "You!" and pointed to me get up there right now. So, I listened to him and I went up to the altar, and bam! I was suddenly slain in the spirit and found myself on the floor laying on my back. I tried to look up, but this bright light kept pushing me down. I did remember all the older women, grandma types, standing all around me praying for me in the Spirit. What a trippy feeling! And that night I received Jesus Christ as my Lord and Savior,

After a while, service was over, and Paul and I went home. We started attending services, usually as a family, continuously. I still could not stop fighting my weed habit and meth habit. One night pastor called us up to pray and all of a sudden in the Spirit, JESUS came down and hugged me. Pastor Maiden saw it and he said, "Mike's feeling something, aren't you?"

I said, "Yes" and started mumbling, Pastor said what, I yelled, "JESUS JUST CAME DOWN AND HUGGED ME!"

He shot down from the heavenlies like those 4th of July sparkles you light with a match. The church just started praising GOD!

Matthew 26:4-
*Watch and Pray, that you enter not in temptation: the spirit indeed is willing, but the flesh is week.*

Well, I was 29 years-old and the Lord started dealing with me to get married. Darlene's daughter left to go back to Pearl, Mississippi, so she left and I think a couple of weeks later I asked Darlene to marry me. She said yes, so we went up to the high desert to Hesperia, to their wedding chapel. Before we went though, we did a couple of lines of meth and smoked 3 joints, I remember taking our vows and almost started busting up laughing.

Anyway, when we got home something felt a lot different, especially that night on our honeymoon. It was like a weight was lifted off our shoulders because the Lord honored us for fulfilling his word when it came to the marriage vows and making that covenant with him as the word said in the Bible.

We always wanted to rent a house, so we found one in Rialto, CA. It was about 10 miles east of where we were living. It was a dive, but when you're a drug addict and wanting to try to better your life, we thought this was it. It had an empty built-in swimming pool that was full of crap and stagnant water boards. The boys and I would try to play whiffle ball around it. We had a blast!

Rent was $650.00 a month. There was one thing about this house: In my opinion, it was possessed. At times we could see black objects floating around. Now was it the drugs or demons?

There was a front bedroom that no one would sleep in because of some story of an alcoholic uncle that died in there. Anyway, we kept on going to church and a lady from there wanted us to mentor her. I remember Darlene and I were fighting and arguing so bad one day when she showed up. We tried to hide the front and she didn't stay long. We couldn't even take care of ourselves, never mind helping somebody else out. LOL!

Gary started not feeling well, so we brought him to the hospital at Loma Linda University. He was diagnosed with viral spinal meningitis, and he was very sick. We were there for days, and we even had our drug dealer deliver meth to the parking lot, just so we could keep awake. We called the church for prayer.

Remember folks, when you receive Jesus Christ as your Lord and Savior, HE IS NOT A MAGIC WAND! You will have trials and tribulations spiritually because there is an adversary out there. Also, when you get born again, it is your spirit that gets reborn, not your flesh. You have to work on that.

1 PETER 5:8-
*BE SOBER, be vigilant; because your adversary the devil, AS a roaring lion, walks about seeking whom he may devour.*
*Amen.*

Well, the prayers were working. Within a week, Gary was home and resting. We were struggling even to make that $650.00 a month payment. But one weekend, close to crunch time when all the bills were due, my friend Lance came over and brought a bunch of food. We barbecued and he dropped $2000.00 cash down, and about 3 ounces of weed. Heck, we even had enough food to eat for the rest of the week.

It was getting to where California was NOT working anymore. Darlene's sister had moved to Iowa and we were thinking about it. Darlene and I were still fighting and arguing a lot, and one day we decided to watch TBN. There was a preacher on there named Mario Murillo. As we were watching, he stared right through that T.V. screen and said, "I'm sensing something in the

Spirit. There are two people out there that love each other dearly, and you two have been at each other's throats with much arguing and fighting."

Darlene and I looked at each other and I said, "He's talking about us."

Remember that house we lived in had many demonic spirits in the first place? And we knew nothing about spiritual warfare like we do now.

Things were still not working for us in California. The 1992 Presidential Election was upon us, so we decided to pack up and move. I called Pastor Maiden and told him we were moving. He asked why we were doing that. I told him there was nothing for us there anymore and said that I'd be in touch.

Proverbs 3:5-6-

*Trust in the Lord with all your heart, and lean NOT unto your own understanding. In all your ways acknowledge him, and he shall direct your paths.*

So, we loaded up a travel trailer from U-HAUL with only very little furniture and a bunch of clothes, and of course my weed. LOL. We only had $700.00 on this journey from Rialto, CA to Fort Dodge, Iowa.

We headed out up through the High Desert to Las Vegas, NV, and then to Interstate 80. We decided to stop at the Aladdin Hotel and Casino there and we ran into a so-called friend, Dale. He was working there, and in the past, he tried dating my wife, Darlene, but it was cool. We were married and I wasn't going there. He did give us a meal card to eat free. After we had bought our room for the night, we played very little on the dime machines and lost a little and won a little. We had to rest because Darlene and I were coming down hard off the meth, so we had to sleep and eat. That's why we didn't make it 5 hours on the road when we first journeyed out.

Well, we woke had a big breakfast, and drove up Interstate 15 to Interstate 80. We were getting restless and tired after driving for hours. We were trying to make it to Sydney, Nebraska to Gary's grandmother's house. We made it, spent the night, and Bryce and Jean gave us a great big breakfast after a great roast beef dinner from one of his cattle.

We got back on I-80 and traveled from one end of cornhusker land to the other. We were set to drive into Iowa, but our car broke down and we ran out of money. We pulled into this rest stop and a trucker helped us get our car going. I think it was the alternator. Darlene called her old boss in California, Mr. Fox, for his gas card number. We filled the tank and got going again.

Right when we traveled to the fork to interchange, the boys and I started getting into an argument. Gary started kicking the back of my seat and I ended up locking them up and nutting up. I was gonna kick the crap out of them, Which I started to do.

*Mike and Darlene*

*Mike with Led Zeppelin Poster*

*Photo of Crash from News Article, June 25, 1980*

# POLICE
## BRIEFS

### Truck driver injured

NORMAN — A 40-year-old Norman man was listed in serious condition Friday at Norman Regional Hospital after the cement truck he was driving rolled at Porter Avenue and Tecumseh Road.

Lt. Glenn Dobry said Michael Luciani was pinned in the truck's cab for several minutes before emergency workers could free him.

The one-vehicle accident occurred about 7:50 a.m. and blocked traffic on both lanes of Porter Avenue, Dobry said. The rollover caused traffic to be detoured to Franklin Road and Rock Creek Road.

### Morning accident

Transcript Photo by **Joshua Pace**

A cement truck overturned while southbound near the corner of North Porter Avenue and Tecumseh Road at about 7:30 a.m. Friday, Norman police officers who responded to the accident reported. Norman firefighters also were on the scene and said the driver had to be cut free. The truck's driver was taken to Norman Regional Hospital, where he was listed in serious condition. There has been no official statement from the police department on the cause of the crash; however, dense fog-like conditions could have been a contributing factor.

*News Article, March 14, 2003*

Darlene got out of the car screaming, "Help, help. Help!"

The U-haul trailer was all tweaked but did not come undone. Remember, this was the non-cell phone era. I chilled out and lit one up. I think it was a bunch of roach weed I had left. I got high and didn't talk to anyone for hours.

After hitting the 29 Interstate, we drove up the state of Iowa. We finally drove into Fort Dodge, Iowa. Darlene's sister, Jeannie met us there around sunset. It seemed forever to get to their house in Clare, Iowa, but we made it. We were all burned out. It was November 1992. Darlene & I made it upstairs to the bedroom. It was drafty and cold, but we were so tired, we fell fast asleep. It was a blessing that Steve and Jeannie let us land there.

The next morning when we woke up, it was like, "Where are we?"

Darlene started hating it on day one. We were broke, busted, and disgusted. We were still trying to get that poison out of our system,

Well, a couple of days went by, and we needed cash and weed fast. I called the insurance company for a back injury for a $ 1000.00 advance and they sent it to me. What a blessing! I got it in about 4 days, but when it came, I had to use some of it for some room and board and food. I paid Mr. Fox back, and after a couple of days,

I was geetering for weed. Well Jeannie knew someone in Otho, Iowa, so I drove down there right past the sheriff and got my ¼ ounce and got out of there. Otho was a town about 500 people.

So, I was getting high now that I had my chill pill. About a week went by, and we had been wanting our own place so bad. I called the insurance company again and this time I asked for $2000.00 and they sent it.

*Matthew 7:7-8* Ask, and it shall be given to you seek, and you shall find, knock, and it shall be opened unto you. For every one that asks receives, and he that seeks shall find, and to him, that knocks shall be opened.

Darlene and I went looking for a place and we found a house for $350.00 a month- not bad! Now all we needed were jobs to pay the bills. We were getting a little bit of government assets, what I called government cheese (food stamps, HEAP, these were drug addicts' dream.) I always had more money for my weed and speed, LOL!

We were trying really bad to get over that hump of NOT geetering, (slang word for meth) but we did contact our old drug dealers a couple times. We were burning out on the stuff, but not the weed. Anyway, we did the meth that came, but we were not feeling too good. I remember one time when it came, our car broke down and our brother-in-law, Steve, came by to check it out. We were so high on meth that we could not comprehend. We could not get it fixed. Darlene hated that place wanted to go back to California. We finally came down off the meth and stopped for a while.

We needed a car and had very little money. Rudy was coming over to give us a ride to look for a car. He was our niece, Julie's, husband. Darlene told us to go up the road where Randall's was. It was our local grocery store. We looked to the left of the parking lot and there was a white Buick for sale. We went in and talked to the lady that owned it. She worked at the courtesy booth. We agreed to meet with her when she got off work to test drive it. We did and it drove nicely. The reason she and her husband were selling it was that they had bought a newer vehicle. She wanted $500.00 for it I asked her if she would take $400.00. She said yes.

Darlene had told me she had a dream that night that there would be a car at the Randall's parking lot. We just started praising God, because we had a good running car locally.

We had applied for HUD and did get approved, but the house we were living in did not accept it. So, we moved to a duplex a couple of miles downtown, across from the Y.M.C.A. and Leo's Auto Sales. He was our landlord and a good guy. He liked the government cheese checks also. LOL!

We lived there a little bit over a year. The boys and I would go over to the Y and play a lot of basketball. Still looking for work, I decided to go get my Class B driver's license and all of my school bus endorsements, which I did. John, the guy that I first got my weed off of in Otho, came by a few nights later asked if we wanted some meth. He opened up his hand and had an eightball, all flaked ready to go. Darlene and I both looked at each other and said, "NO THANKS!"

I did say, "Do you have a joint, though?" he gave me a pinner I smoked it. John went into the basement and shot up. I smoked the joint. John left, and Darlene and I went to bed. We prayed and we just started praising God and thanking him he finally took the meth away from us.

At the same time, Dora, Darlene's daughter, needed to get out of Pearl, Mississippi, so we needed a bigger place. She came and stayed with us, but it was crowded. HUD told us they had a big two-story, four-bedroom house. We nailed it. Since the meth geeter days were done and gone, I decided to go apply at the Fort Dodge school system and they hired me as a sub driver. Darlene had a few part-time jobs: the deli counter at Randall's and then at a cleaners.

We moved into the big house and I started meeting people-GOOD people! Mitch and Sandy, and Maury and Carol. Mitch and Sandy helped us get our first washer and dryer. Carol ran a candle shop out of her house, and Maury had an alternator shop. He always had connections with $100.00 vehicles that were rust buckets, of which I bought two. One was a blue Toyota. It had been rear-ended and someone had put license plates and mounted taillights on them. The boys were embarrassed to ride in it with me. The horizon we bought was yellow.

I was driving the school bus for a year and a half, and to supplement the income I worked at Fort Dodge High School as a hall monitor. I would also have some good road trips with sports teams when they had away games, basketball, baseball, swimming, and whenever there was basically any event that popped up and it was my turn on the rotation list. Also, the bus driver always ate for free as a courtesy. It paid the bills.

I also had a part-time job at night driving to Marshalltown, IOWA for APAC, which was a telemarketing company, delivering tapes and documents. This job lasted about 4 months before the company went out of business.

Well, with summer coming and school out, I needed my weed. My friend Lance would send me some killer Humbolt weed. I picked up a part-time job for the summer umpiring baseball for the Y.M.C.A. youth leagues and also for the high school games. It paid good, but I was still getting high smoking weed.

With about 2 and a half weeks to go before the start of my second school season, I started drinking a gallon of water a day because during the baseball season, I was smoking weed all summer, so I quit. On the second day of the new school year, my number came up for a drug test. I remember Pete, the mechanic, drove me down to the clinic to do my urine test. I was freaking out! Inside of me was screaming, "I'm busted!"

I called Darlene and told her what happened. I finally started praying to God, "If you could just get me out of this one," and He did. And the funny thing about it, I don't even remember trying to make a deal with him because I knew, and He always knows that I would blow it again. LOL!

I always wondered why my number came up and nobody else did, then I remembered my neighbor, Pat, had a little daughter that I drove on my bus route. We had been smoking a lot all summer with Pat, but I never looked back at that hunch. It would have still been on me anyway.

Fall was coming and with another winter not too far in the distance, practically every night the boys and I would run across the street to the Y.M.C.A. to play basketball. We had great full-court games with high schoolers and adults. It was the only thing to do in that godforsaken town. I thought, "It sure is funny how we always want God when we think we are in trouble."

I remember one night playing, and this big kid that was taller and bigger than me just kept talking smack and wouldn't shut up. I finally got so mad, I pinned him up against the wall and slapped him real hard and grabbed his neck. Paul said, "What are you doing? That kid is only 15 years old!" Oh boy, we both apologized and moved on. I thought he was in his thirties!

Another winter had passed, and Darlene and I were really starting to hate this place more and more. We were praying more and more for God to guide us out of this place, Fort Dodge, IOWA.

I finally got off the bus route and my teacher associate job, and there came an opening for a food service van driver. I applied and when I walked in for the interview, it was the principal at Duncombe Elementary School interviewing me. "What a GOD thing!" I thought. This guy used to watch me play whiffle ball with the boys and the neighborhood kids outside the school.

Well, I got the job from 6 a.m. to 2:30 p,m, Monday through Friday. It was tax time around 1996 when we filed and got a refund of $845.00. I said, "Yeah!" but a funny thing happened about a week later. Another tax check came for about $850.00 I called the IRS because I thought there was a mistake. They said, no, it was back overpayment on my child support in California. PRAISE GOD!

Around Christmas time, I remember Darlene coming down the stairs and asked me if there was a Norman in Oklahoma. I said, "Yup, home of the Sooners."

She said, "What's a Sooner?" LOL! All I remembered was telling her, "Why? What's God saying?" She just felt it in her Spirit it was time to move on. We wrote to the Norman Chamber of Commerce for information. We also wrote to Seattle, Kansas City, and I think somewhere in Florida. A couple of weeks later, we heard from Norman Chamber of Commerce and received visitor packet from them. They also sent the $3.00 back for the newspaper. So, there it was, our so-called sign to get out. Around Feb. 1997, I started telling people at my job. WRONG MOVE! I was being treated like crap all around the block in that godforsaken city. I had so much doubt and unbelief. I didn't know at that time because my spiritual growth in the Lord was at a big fat zero on the discernment scale, LOL! People were being so rotten and mean everywhere. So much fear and jealousy. It was horrible, but we were going through with it.

We drove a bright yellow Horizon. I couldn't leave with that, so a so-called mechanic friend we knew had an Audi. We bought it for $850.00. It looked great and ran okay, but, you see where I'm going here with this? All hydraulic burn.

I gave my job notice and on March 5th. I went down to Ron's carwash. That's where U-haul was also. We got a 24-ft. truck and a trailer to haul the Audi. As I was paying for everything, the devil had one more dig. Ron asked me where I was going, and I told him Oklahoma. He said, "You'll be back."

I said, "What? Not me. We are not from here."

He said, "You will be back. They always come back."

I said, "Nope, not me!" Well, it's been 23 years and I went back for a visit to see family in Council Bluffs. We packed up the night before on March 6th, 1997, and headed to Oklahoma.

*Hebrews 13:14 KJV*-For here we have no continuing city, But we seek one to come.

It was Darlene, Gary, and I moving to Oklahoma. Gary is our youngest son. Our daughter, Dora, had gotten married to her husband, David. Our son, Paul, was with a woman named Ericka, and they were expecting a baby. So, we left that part of our family behind.

On March 7th, we headed out of Fort Dodge, Iowa and drove down Highway 20 to I-35 South. We would drive until we got down to Wichita, KS. We found a hotel and right next door was a Chinese restaurant. We ate a great dinner and fell asleep. We got up the next morning around 7:00 am and drove around 6 hours.

We finally landed in Norman on March 8th, on Main St. and I-35. The motel, I think at the time, was Econo Lodge. We got settled in and spent the night. I think the first place we went to eat was Taco Bell. They didn't have one in Fort Dodge, Iowa at the time. We then got up early in the morning and got a newspaper to start looking for houses to rent.

We found one and we brought our HUD certificate. The landlord took it, but on our way to look at the house, our great beast car, our Audi, broke down in front of it. A lady came out to us and offered a phone we could use. Her name was Bonnie, and what a blessing she was. She became a great neighbor. Come to find out, it was the hydraulic brake system and very expensive to fix. We rigged it up after we moved in and traded it for a chevy Corsica 4-door from Womack Auto Sales on Porter Avenue. It was American with a dented door, but, what the heck? We had transportation.

We moved onto Richmond Drive the next day. I started looking for churches. I found one called Christian Center Church that I visited. I sat during the Wednesday service. As the church service was over, an older woman sitting behind me asked, "What is your name, brother?"

I told her our story and that we just moved down from Iowa. Come to find out, she was the pastor's mother. She started that church and handed it over to him. Her name was Norma Jean Hildebrand. Who would have thought she would be the pastor of Darlene and me down the road.

Well, we needed a blessing. We were watching TBN and we decided to bless a certain Ministry with our last

$100. Well, I needed it quick, so I thought I would be at the front door for 2 weeks trying to chase the mailman down, yet nothing came. I thought my faith was there but couldn't hang. Nothing came. I was still smoking weed, but I felt in my spirit I was getting close to stopping.

Well, then came job hunting, and I found one right away. When I found out 80 % of the people in the organization were homosexuals I quit. My spiritual growth in the Lord and my love walk was not even close to where the Lord wanted me to be at that time in my walk with Him.

While job hunting was still going on, Darlene had a half-sister in Oklahoma City that we finally hooked up with. They kept asking why we didn't contact them earlier. We just told them we wanted to make it on our own.

A job finally popped up with Basset Mattress Factory. They were looking for a class B truck driver, so I applied for the job and they hired me. I would be delivering mattress sets to all of the Sight and Sound stores throughout Oklahoma and surrounding states. And believe me, after a month of eating rice and beans, this was a blessing started at $7.50 an hour. Right when I reported to HUD they kicked us off.

We started going to church regularly. Darlene ran an ad in the newspaper to do cleaning and people started calling to book her. At the same time, her niece, Donna had bought a new car and asked us if we wanted to buy her old one. It was a 1986 Honda Accord with about 80,000 miles on it and only had one owner. What a blessing! She wanted a $1000.00 for it, so we put $500 down, and she let Darlene work off the rest by cleaning her house. Now we had 2 cars so we could both go to work.

Things were coming together nicely, and I was learning the state of Oklahoma really well from driving on my job. However, our rent was still a little steep for our budget. And of course, I was still smoking weed. That job did not drug test me, but I was mostly smoking in the evening and weekends. I was getting so burned out on it. Darlene was looking for a more affordable house and I was still working. In the meantime, Paul, Ericka, and baby Bailey had moved down to be with us.

On one particular weekend of September 1997, I came home on a Friday night, the 12th. We started partying, and Paul and I were smoking maple syrup blunts. We woke up Saturday, on the 13th, and started smoking heavily again. By this time, I was getting so sick in my spirit and I wanted to stop so badly. We had half of the blunt left. I went to my bedroom and I remember it like yesterday, I just laid back on my bed and screamed to the heavens, "PLEASE GOD, TAKE THIS FROM ME!"

I fell asleep for about 2 hours and when I woke up, Paul asked me if I wanted to finish smoking the blunt.

I said, "No."

He said, "What?"

I told him, "I'm done!"

GOD finally took it from me after 25 years, the drug of my choice. Never had a relapse or anything. This is so GOOD how our heavenly Father is. No matter what job I had in the future, I always passed a drug test, all to the glory of God! Thank you, Jesus!

About a week went by, and Darlene found a house on the corner of Eufaula and Stewart Streets in Norman. There is a basketball court there now, and boys and girls club on Emanuel Baptist Church Property. Sheryl was the receptionist at the church, and she rented Darlene the 3-bedroom house for $400.00 a month. She was such a blessing to us, and the pastor was also. We ended up living there for 3 years.

Things were going pretty smoothly. We were both working going to church. The end of the year was approaching. Norma Jean called, and she invited us to her home for Christmas Eve dinner. We only told Pastor Derek and he told us the Lord must have told her something about us because she was a stickler preacher and evangelist. She would never invite anybody to her home. That was her sanctuary. We thought we were being blessed, and a very high honor, so we went.

We were at the table eating dinner, Darlene and I were there with her family, and she asked me, "What's your story, Mike?"

Well, right then and there as I started giving my testimony. Their jaws dropped, but they were not surprised. We had a good evening, hung out, had dessert, opened gifts, and Darlene and I went home. We were still working and did not care about the New Years' service or religious tradition where people would get together and take communion. Which was all good to us.

1998 was here and Darlene and I continued to work. Norma Jean came to us about opening a storefront church up in Oklahoma City on 89th and Western, inside the Brookwood Village strip mall. So one evening, Darlene and I met her up at the building along with 4 others: Her son, Kirk, and his wife, Shonda, would be part of the praise and worship team. Al and Ginger would be our associate pastors. As for Darlene and me, no clue! We were just there! (But we believe to this day God was preparing us, for what? Only heaven knows!)

We started going faithfully. The first year was powerful! I used to sit in the back with the kids clowning around. One Sunday service, we had guest speakers from Kenya, Africa. Their names were Clifton and Lita McDowell and they lived here in the states but were missionaries in Africa.

Clifton was preaching he looked back at me and told me, "Mike, the Lord just told me to tell you that you are going to be used to reach people in hard-to-reach areas."

At the time, I did not put two and two together until weeks later. Darlene and I were talking, and she said, "Don't you remember that same word from the folks that had come over to see how we were doing in California from Hosanna Christian fellowship Redlands California?"

I said, "Oh yeah, I remember that now!"

What a blessing! The same word from the Lord, in two different states, almost ten years apart.

I finally found a job delivering lumber for Hope Lumber Company in Norman after the mattress company. I will always remember that spring to fall that year of 1998. It was about 105 degrees every day. People kept telling us it was very unusual.

That job didn't work out after a year, but I liked it and I met one of my best friends, Robby. And to this day, I have known him the longest. I knew we were going to hit it off when I got off the truck one day after delivery. I had my Red Sox t-shirt on, and he was a Cubs fan, so back then, you see where I'm going with this? We were both doomed with our beloved franchise! It's funny, I kept telling him over and over, "One day, my Red Sox are going to win it!" And who would have thought they would win 4 and the cubbies got there once!

Well, that job went south, but I have kept in touch with Robby ever since, and his cool wife, Shari. We should both be so lucky and blessed to have two great women in our lives that keep us both in line.

The church was going well. The old foreman at Bassett Mattress was now working for Mathis Brothers, Lady Americana Mattresses. He called and told me they were looking for a class B truck Driver, so I took the job. It paid about $8.50 an hour for basically the same gig as Bassett. Different stores, but same delivery area. It went well for a while, Monte, the one that got me the job, started to become a snitch on every move that any of us employees made. I quit after about a year there.

One day I was home watching the news and saw that Monte was walking in the alley in between the Lady Americana Factory and Factory Direct Furniture when he got nailed by a worker speeding down the alley. He flew right up in the air and both legs were broken plus a lot more injuries. Was it payback? I remember going to visit him a couple of times during his healing process and we remained friends over the next couple of years.

One Sunday evening at our Eufaula house, I was in the bedroom and all of a sudden, I heard a smashing sound. I ran to the front door and opened it and my windshield on my Accord was smashed in with a roofing hammer. I could tell by the ridges on the imprint from the hammer. I was freaked out and I thought it was a revenge payback for what one of my sons did to someone. But what the devil meant for bad, God turned it into good. My Pastor, Norma Jean, called a couple of weeks later and told me to bring it to Metro Glass in Norman. She wanted to bless me with a new windshield. That was cool and I always remembered our local yellow pages had a coupon section. I found a coupon for 25% off the final bill which was a little bit under $200. Praise God! Norma Jean was always a blessing to everyone she came in contact with. Amen.

I was going through the fire with employment. I thought to myself If I could keep a job for over a year maybe I will make it with the spirit of offense and or anger or maybe it was because I wasn't smoking weed for a few years because during the baby Christian walk that was still at times my chill pill. Lol.

Well, I was back on the unemployment scene, so every Sunday I would get the classified ads to look for a job. I saw an ad that Norman Concrete was looking for drivers with a class B driver's license with air brake endorsement. I had them both, so I applied. Tom, the plant manager, called me, so I went to the interview. He sent me to do a physical and take a drug test. I passed them both, and he hired me. Well, morning came, and that spirit of fear hit me. I did not want to go, I think because in the back of my mind, I had never driven a concrete mixer. So, my beautiful, wonderful wife started calling me names and told me to get out of the house and go try it or she was going to kick my butt!

So, I went, and when I showed up, Tom was such a blessing. He was a very humble man and was taking his time with showing me the ropes slowly. He was sending me out with experienced drivers and things were going well.

It was Nov 1999. One long, cold winter was coming, and with concrete being seasonal work, it could be brutal. It started to be a blessing. I would meet some cool people, and some not so cool, but that's the name of the game in any business. I really started enjoying this job the more I got used to it.

Our son Paul was up in Iowa and he was having family problems. Our youngest son, Gary, was starting to be rebellious and get into trouble. While we were trying to get Gary straightened up, Paul's wife kicked him out. He had no place to go, so Dora drove from Rockwell City, Iowa to get him. Then Darlene and I drove from Oklahoma up to Iowa to get him to bring him back with us. Both boys would not comply with the house rules, so to make a long story short, they would both run out of favor and run from the law. So deep down, Darlene and I knew we were supposed to be called to Norman because all hell was breaking loose around us.

2 Timothy 1:7-

*But GOD did not give us a spirit of fear, but of power, and love, and of a sound mind.*

My job was going great and Norman concrete was in the process of selling to Martin Merrietta Materials. Less than a year later, they sold it to Schwarz Ready Mix. It was about this time that the pastor from the church that we were renting the house from came over one day and told us we had to move. They wanted to use the house for the youth group. He thought we were going to be all upset, but Darlene told him, "Praise God!" because the Lord was telling her in her spirit that he wanted us to move on. He was relieved that we weren't upset. We had been praying for God to open a door for us to buy a house.

So, Darlene started to look for places to rent. She found one, so we went and looked at it. It was ok, but too small. The owners asked what we were looking for. We told them what we wanted. For about a year, we had been asking the Lord for a house with a two-car garage and a fireplace.

He said, "I may have something."

We drove up to Quanah Parker Trail and fell in love with it, but it was for sale, not a rental. We told them we wanted to buy, all done by faith. We had never been homeowners, but when the clock was ticking, we had favor from God. Every obstacle that came against us, the Lord's hand was there. The money came in for this part of the contract and that part. Family members were blessing us, and the last part of the money we needed, dad and mom sent without even asking, And on March 22, 2001. We were homeowners. Praise God!

1 Peter 4:12-
*Beloved think it not strange concerning the fiery trial which is to try you, as though some strange thing happened unto you.*

Things were going pretty well. Darlene and I were both working. I had been with the Concrete Company for almost 3 years, even though it changed names 3 times. I had some vacation time built up and Darlene and I always wanted to go to a Kenneth Copeland Convention. There was one coming up in Branson, Missouri. Early march of 2003, I managed to get 6 days off, we took off on a Thursday and made it to Branson that evening. We had made reservations, so we had a beautiful room even our dog, Chance, loved it. He was our little beloved rat terrier. He lived to be 18 ½ years old until his passing.

Friday morning came and we went to the morning and evening service. After talking to a few people, it was like a competition of how many times they would flock to these events. It was okay, but something was unsettling in my spirit, but I had no clue as to why. All I know is that I could feel the presence of God. We went back Saturday morning, and it was okay. When the evening service came around, we went back, but Darlene decided to go back to the hotel. She was tired, so I told her I would be up in a bit.

Well song service started. It was Len Minks, the popular gospel singer. It started ok, but all of a sudden, things moved in slow motion, I looked up to the right side of the building and there was this black part of the wall. This went on for about 50 seconds. Then I heard the voice of the Lord, Jesus, and he specifically told me, "Mike, do not walk ahead of me or behind me. I want to walk with you, side by side, together.

Then, everything came back to its original format. I stayed about 30 minutes. I couldn't get into it. I was tired and when I got back to the hotel, Darlene was just getting up and she was hungry. It was about 10:30, but we found a Domino's Pizza that was open. As the church service was getting out, the pizza man was delivering our pizza. A few people on the balconies going back to their rooms and they asked how we got that. The pizza guy told me they were closing at 11. God was even watching over us in that special pizza moment. LOL!

Sunday morning came and we had had enough, so we got up and headed back to Norman,

My sister, Beth, and her husband, Jim, were driving cross country moving to New York state with my nephews, Sean and Eddie. Monday, Tuesday, and Wednesday came and went. We had a great visit. I had to be back to work on Thursday. That was rough, but I made it.

The next day was Friday, March 14. It was a very, very foggy morning. We had to be in at 4 a.m., but concrete delivery was on hold because of the weather. I remember sleeping in my little Honda Accord for a couple of hours. About 7 a.m., they started firing up the mixers. My Peterbilt truck was down from the day before due to an air pod cylinder, so the part had to be ordered for repair. One of the mechanics was working on a truck for me to use. I vaguely remember he was tightening something in the back of the loaner mixer I was to use. We heard over the radio from other plants that there were a couple of mishaps.

It was my turn, so I filled up my water tank. I was to take a 10-yard load down to Alameda and Vicksburg in Norman. I headed east on Tecumseh Rd. I was doing about 25 MPH in a 50 zone, and I could not see anything in front of me. All of a sudden, I came upon a stop sign and hit the brakes. I slid through the T-shaped road at Porter Ave. I did not want to roll downhill into trees, so I made a right turn and over I went. I could not pivot my left leg, it was broken at the knee. The left side of my face was covered in glass. I remember grabbing the radio mike and yelling help 4 times.

The first one on the scene was an OU med student taking my vitals and then a retired officer came on the scene. I was trapped for about 35 minutes. The rescue team was called to the west side of Tecumseh Road, but I was on the east side. They finally made it and had to use the jaws of life to cut me out.

The ambulance brought me to Norman Regional to the emergency room. Darlene met me there in the ER. I was in so much pain. The doctors were looking at me while an officer from the Norman police station was trying to write me a citation. I started cussing him up a storm and told him to get the heck out of there. My boss and Darlene rushed in and Darlene asked the officer what was going on.

He replied, "I'm writing Michael up a citation for the accident." Darlene told him to leave, and he said he would mail it.

I did not even have any test done on my body. I was in so much pain. The orderlies finally took me down to get a cat scan, and when they put me on that hard surface it felt like they just threw me there. Finally, after they were done with the scan they brought me back to the ER. There they were waiting on the results to come back.

They finally came back, and it was evident that I needed surgery. I was diagnosed with a punctured lung, collapsed lung, 16 broken ribs, and if it wasn't for my boss telling the doctor about my broken left knee, I'd probably be dragging my left leg around. They told Darlene I needed surgery, and since my knee was broken, the doctor said he would put me out on anesthesia so I wouldn't feel the chest tubes going in the side of my chest cavities. The Doctors told Darlene that only about 5 percent of people in those types of accidents and with those types of injuries survive.

Once the surgery was done and complete, it was healing time. They put me in the recovery room for a while then in a room. All I remember in that room when I was all morphined-out, was going on a trip and didn't have to leave my room. Someone left the bathroom light and exhaust fan on and I thought I was in Freddie Kruger's boiler room on Nightmare on Elm Street, just from the noise it was making. I remember a couple of times looking up at the wallpaper stripes and it seemed like they were moving around like dancing pixie dust smiling at me.

JOHN 10:10-
*The thief cometh not, but for to steal, and to kill,
and to destroy: I am come that they may have life,
and that they have it more abundantly.*

I was in Norman Regional Hospital about 12 days. I should have stayed longer, but I was NOT a good patient.

I was always complaining that I wanted to go home. The nurses and doctors were great, but I was all drugged up and constantly complaining. I remember this one early morning, I had the chest tubes in my chest, and I was very irritated. I called my wife around 4:30 in the morning and asked her what she was doing, and she said told me she was sleeping.

"Why? What are you doing?" she asked.

I said I was sitting there having a cup of coffee. By then, the nurse had come in the room. My bed was lifted as high as it would go, and I had jumped down and was sitting in the chair with nothing but chest tubes and a washcloth over my private parts. In the meantime, a light bulb went off in my wife's head and said to herself, "He's not drinking coffee right now!"

She rushed down to the hospital and the nurse told her what I did. They were both amazed that I didn't pull the tubes out of my chest and rip the dressing and brace out of my left leg knee. I knew the Lord was starting the healing process.

I hadn't gone to the bathroom (bowel movement) for about 10 days. I finally thought I had to go. I must have sat on this bedpan for 30 seconds, but it took my wife and orderly 30 minutes to get me to sit on it. I was in so much pain. I told everybody that this was not working, so they rushed around the hospital looking for a bedside commode. They found one and it looked like it came out of a preschool. As soon as I sat on it, all the wingnuts went flying like ricochet bullets all over the room. LOL! It was not working. The orderly went and found a bigger one and I finally did what I needed to do.

I finally came home after 12 days, and boy I thought it was a mistake! I wanted out of the hospital so badly. Our brother-in-law, Jim, came over and built a ramp. Pastor Joe from the Lion of Judah Fellowship met us at the house also and they both helped me get inside. I could not lay in the bed because of the broken ribs, so I had to sleep in a recliner for 8 months. I remember when I went to the hospital, it was dreary with no leaves on the trees, but when I came out of the hospital, all the leaves on trees were blooming flowers. It never crossed my mind really until now, the Lord was saying, "New Life with the four seasons I have given you!" Amen! Praise God!

Galatians 5:22-
*But the Fruit of the SPIRIT, is Love, Joy, Peace,*
*Longsuffering, Kindness, Goodness, Faithfulness.*

I always wondered why the Lord put that Long Suffering in there. Well, for the first 8 months after I returned home, I went through that valley of darkness. In the first few months, I got Kidney stones so bad they had to put me back in the hospital. Since I did not have my own health insurance, the urologist had to use old school technology and go up the front of me on my private parts to laser them out.

Well, it worked, but Mr.-Stubborn-me, I wanted to see the Christian rock band, Bleach, because they were coming through town the next day. The doctor told me I could leave the hospital if I ate (Little Caesar's Pizza) and I was urinating properly. I did both. I was in so much pain urinating, it was like leaking shattered glass and cherry Kool-aid. That should have been a sign that I was not ready to leave the hospital. Darlene was pretty upset that I would do this just to go to a concert.

I made it and I was rocking out with Bleach. During all of this, I was talking to a Norman police officer and showing him my hospital bracelet. He called me a trooper and I thought that was cool. Well, I rocked out, but went home in so much pain.

Darlene asked me, "Where are your high-powered antibiotics?"

I told her I forgot them. She went and got them the next day. Within two days, I was back in the hospital with a serious kidney infection. LOL! The moral of that story:

"Please, people. When you're deathly ill and come out of a major vehicle accident, listen to your spouse!"

I was in the hospital for about a week and the Lord healed me through doctors and modern medicine. I was very thankful!

October of 2003, the same year as the accident, I remember it well. It was what the man would call an Indian summer. It was very hot still in Oklahoma leading up to November, and all of a sudden Darlene and I caught the flu. It was brutal! We were both very sick over four months into 2004. We both took turns barely making it out of the house to get supplies and groceries, My body was healing but it was a very slow process.

It was a blessing having people around, but after a couple of months of being home, it was like the world disappeared. I went from $600.00 a week to $265.00 a week on workman's comp with no health insurance. Thank God Darlene was still working.

Both our boys were in trouble with the law. After running for two years in Missouri, they finally came back. It didn't last long before they were both arrested. Paul got two years and Gary would do time in drug court, then go back to Missouri to do more time. We were beside ourselves, but believe it or not, God was still working behind the scenes. As I started to go visit these prison facilities, I would just look around sometimes and talk to inmates and their families when I could get away with it. The Man was pretty strict in their rules, but most of the time cool. We would do this on and off for a few years.

I had more surgeries to get the metal out of my left knee and leg and then shots in my back. It was around Oct. 2006, when I didn't think I could go back to work, but I did. I would drive a bus for Community Action head start program in Oklahoma City for 3 years. It was okay to start but getting paid the last working day of the month was horrible. You had to stretch your dollars, at least for 2 weeks. LOL!

I needed to make more money, so I decided to jump back in the lumber yard for $14.00 an hour. After two days, I had 28 hours, but I just could not do it. My body was too messed up. So, on and on with work. I had 7 jobs in 6 years. The last one let me go, and to me, that was it.

I collected my unemployment while at the same time I filed for my social security disability benefits. After a year and a half, unemployment ran out. It took another 3 years to finally get my S.S.D.I., While I was waiting, it was around the beginning of 2013, I was driving north on Crawford Street and I saw a guy that I use to pour concrete for named Greg Hitchcock. He lived right at the corner of Crawford and Hayes.

He asked me what I was doing, and I said, "Not much."

He asked if I would be interested in prison ministry. After praying about it, the Lord gave me that prophecy from about 10 years ago, that I would be used to reach people in hard-to-reach areas. I said, "Sure."

He told me what process to take and do. March 2013, I went through the process of getting my Department of Correction volunteer's badge in the state of Oklahoma.

A couple of months later, the Lord gave me Wayside Ministry. My old pastor, Joe, and I always talked about it. The Wayside. So, it stuck. I told the Lord, "If I'm going to serve you, I want to do it right."

I also remember, a year after the accident, he gave me my personal tract. I started putting monthly letters going out to a few people, but God was meeting the needs to get me down to McAlester, OK, to Oklahoma State Pen. Home of the general population and H-UNIT (aka-death row.)

The Lord started opening doors. About 6 of us would go down to death row the last Thursday of the month. As time went on, after talking to these guys, I realized that they are actually good people who just made bad choices in their lives.

But the Lord told me that's all he is interested in: SOULS, SOULS, SOULS! I ministered to the most lost criminal element in the history of the state of Oklahoma, but you know the Lord reminded me that no matter what we are all on death row of some sort of another.

2 Timothy 1:8-

*So do NOT be ashamed of the testimony about our Lord or me his prisoner, Rather, join with me in suffering for the gospel, by the power of God.*

Here are a couple of stories that have been in my spirit that I would like to share with you:

One morning I was in the general population in A-unit. As I was walking up the stairs, I saw this man looking out of his cell. As I walked up to him, I said, "Hey buddy, how are you?" and I told him who I was. He told me with a mean mug frown on his face, "I don't need you, I know everything about the bible."

I said, "That's cool," and I told him, "My name is Michael Luciani and I've come in the name of Jesus to pray with you."

He said, "Do you know who I am?"

I looked on the glass and saw his name. I said, "Christopher."

He said again, "Do you know who I am?"

I said, "Christopher."

He was adamant and he yelled, "I have been on Lock-up Raw on MSNBC in Colorado and New Mexico!"

I said, "No, I have never seen you, man. I just know the Lord told me to come and pray with you."

He said NO and that he knew everything about the Bible.

I said, "Okay, put your hand up here on the glass."

He said, "What?"

I said, "Put your hand on the glass and put it up against mine."

He said, "Why?"

I told him, "You said you know everything about the Bible. Pray for me. I need a financial miracle."

Well, Christopher prayed with me this awesome beautiful prayer for my finances. That was a Thursday, and the following Tuesday I received a check for $200.00 in the mail.

A couple of weeks went by, and late one Saturday night into Sunday morning, I couldn't sleep, so I put on the television. As I was channel surfing, I came across repeats on Lockup Raw, and there he was my friend, Christopher. He was being used as a prop to practice for the man, because his wrist was so skinny, he kept on breaking out of his handcuffs. You could tell the sheriffs were kind of afraid of him, and as the narrator was going on, they were talking about his charges. I guess he had stabbed an inmate or sheriff with a watermelon Jolly Rancher Stix. He had sharpened it up like a knife and stuck one of them. Talk about a God thing, the Lord letting me see this, which would be good for the next month when I would see him again.

Well, God was moving. I had called Dr.Cavallaro and asked him about the old Berry House, which was the Oklahoma juvenile detention center in Oklahoma City. I applied and waited and waited for a response. I finally got ahold of the director and he told me that, no, I could not come in because of my past record. (Who would have thought a 30-year-old record in California would haunt me?)

I called the San Bernardino county court, and they found it. I asked them to mail me a copy and they did. I gave it to Dr. Cavallaro, and he passed it on to the director at the Berry House. After careful consideration, they approved me to come minister to the teenage boys and a couple of times to the girls. It was such a blessing to see some of them being delivered, and some of their spirits breaking to finally let God be God in some of their lives.

Well, the juvie is still going strong. It used to be Tuesdays at 4:00 p.m., but with people leaving and the changing of the guard, so to speak, they moved it to Fridays at 1:00 p.m. Such a blessing how the Lord moved to make it even more convenient to fit my schedule. Amen!

The first couple of months were going great, then all of a sudden, God opened more doors. Dr.Cavallaro received a call from the Oklahoma County Jail. At the time they were housing D.O.C. (department of corrections) inmates there. Chaplain Don asked us if we would come in on Friday afternoons at 3 p.m. for a couple of hours. We were to teach on Destination: Character, The Process of God's Transforming Grace. It was a study guide on how an individual could help the men on transforming their lives and spirit man through Prayer and God's Word.

It was such a blessing. As Dr. Cavallaro was going through the program, the Lord had me watching individuals, and as I was led by the spirit, I would pray for the guys and at times they would break and you could see the love of God just touch them and their spirits. Some would cry, others would say, "How did you know that?" I told them it was the Holy Spirit. We were all amazed.

Well, that went on for about 3 years. We would continue to go down to death row. I did find Christopher in the general population again, and it was a blessing. He was so happy to see me, especially when I told him about the $200.00 I received after he prayed. He also laughed at me when I told him I had seen the rerun on MSNBC Lockup Raw. I asked him jokingly, "What are you doing with that watermelon stix and stabbing people? Those are my favorite Jolly Ranchers!"

He laughed and started showing pictures of his girl-friend and a big church in Tennessee. He told me he would be going there once he got released. This time he let me pray with him and we did. We were both touched by the Holy Spirit. I went on to other cells and the following month he was gone. He was transferred to who knows where.

Another door was opening at the Cleveland County Jail every Sunday. From 1:00-3:00 we would go right into the pods where the guys would sleep, eat, and shower. What a blessing, and sometimes a curse because of some of those demonic spirits in there, but mostly good guys that made terrible choices.

We were doing that frequently but the religious man in charge with his legalistic rules kept busting my chops, especially when I would go into the religious store where he worked to buy my music. However, the Lord kept on telling me to love on this guy, and for a year, I did. The ministry was growing, and I was beginning to think I had bitten off more than I could chew. It was Sundays, Tuesdays, Fridays, and the 3rd Thursday of every month to McAlester, Oklahoma, O.S.P. (Oklahoma State Penitentiary) death row. I was getting burned out fast.

2 Corinthians 3:17-
*Now the Lord is that Spirit, and where the Spirit of the Lord is there is Liberty.*

I kept on moving for the Lord, but I started having problems with the religious man at the Cleveland County Jail as far as the do's, and don'ts of his Church of

Christ religious policy, He also worked part-time at the religious bookstore in town. We clashed personalities a few times, but I was done.

So, Cleveland County Jail was on hold for me a while. For about a year, I would run into him as I would buy my materials at the store where he worked. The Lord told me just to chill out and be nice, so I did for a year.

In the meantime, I was headed back to O.S.P. death row one Thursday in 2016. I came out of the SW pod, and as I came out, there was a metal detector chair there. I was tired and we had about 30 minutes to kill, so I thought I would rest until we had to go back up before leaving to head back to Norman. All of a sudden, the Lord told me to go down to the NE pod.

I told him, "NO! I'm tired," he then spoke to my spirit again and he told me to go down to the NE pod.

I said, "NO!" All of a sudden, he told me again, "I'm NOT going to ask you a third time," so I got off my butt and headed to the NE pod. As I was walking up, it was like the guard knew I was coming. The gate just opened up and closed as I walked through it. I made a right through two more gates, and then a left. I walked all the way down to the end of the pod. On the right, there was a big black guy covered in tattoos, and two Indian guys that were also covered in tattoos. BIG guys!

They looked at me and were startled for a second. I said, "What's up dudes? I'm Michael Luciani from Wayside Ministry and I've come to pray with you. The black guy said, "NO THANKS! I don't need a religion."

I said neither do I. I've come to pray for you and your families. Well, the black guy said, "Okay."

I said, "Put your hand up on the glass part of the cell door."

He did, and right when I started praying for him, you could hear this hollow echo screaming at the top of its lungs. I thought to myself for a second that sounds like ole slew foot, the devil. I looked over and it wasn't the Indian dudes, they were just being disruptive. Finally, the black guy told them to shut up because the man of God was trying to pray, and they listened and did. Everything went at peace for a few seconds, and I told them I had to leave. The Indian guys were banging on their cell doors asking me to pray with them before I left, so I did. It was about 10 minutes till 3:00, and I had to get up top to the entrance of the prison, so we said our goodbyes.

As I was walking back, there were 3 empty cells, and in the middle cell there was a young man's picture on the glass. His name was Jeremy. I kept thinking of the HOLLOW ECHO I heard a few minutes prior. I called out Jeremy's name. I said, "Jeremy, in the name of Jesus, come up here!" It was a darkened cell with no light.

The second time, my voice got louder, and I said, "Jeremy, in the name of Jesus come up here!" (Nothing)

The last time I became spiritually angry, and I said with a firm and loud voice, "JEREMY IN THE NAME OF JESUS, I COMMAND YOU NOW TO COME UP HERE!

All of a sudden, he floated out of nowhere up to the glass door and shouted, "I DON'T WANT TO!" with a screechy demonic, imp voice, and then he floated back into the darkness. I put those two together, the voices and the demonic possession of Jeremy. And that was my very first encounter spiritually with the devil himself. I looked at my watch after that and said, "Time to go. It's 3:00 o'clock." LOL, what a trip! The Lord had me there for such a time as this and he was showing me that obedience is better than sacrifice. Thank God I was obedient!

Ephesians 6:10-12-
*Finally my brethren, be strong in the Lord, and the power of his might. Put on the whole armor of GOD, that ye may be able to stand against the WILES of the DEVIL. For we WRESTLE NOT AGAINST FLESH AND BLOOD, but against, PRINCIPALITIES, against POWERS, against the RULERS, of the DARKNESS of this WORLD, against SPIRITUAL WICKEDNESS in high places.*

As the rest of the year went by, the Oklahoma County Jail was winding down after three years. They were moving all of the department of corrections out and the county would no longer house the inmates. The ministry at the jail was dismantled, so Doc and I moved on. During all this process, there was an inmate that wanted to get married down at O.S.P. for over a year. It was put on hold, and believe it or not, I am a licensed minister.

The inmate whose marriage I was going to officiate, well the public was not too keen on him getting out of death row to go down and get a marriage license, and neither was the victim's family. So, when the Pittsburgh County Court Clerk got wind of this, and the director of the D.O.C., and the Governor, and the news media, guess what? I was totally made the scapegoat.

In Sept of 2016, as I was getting ready for a Dallas trip to go visit my son Gary in prison and to see RED, DISCIPLE, AND SPOKEN in downtown Dallas that same Friday, I received a phone call from O.S.B.I. and on the other side of the phone call, it was an agent wanting me to meet with him on the following Monday.

So, as I started to Dallas, TX. I was pumped and I thought it was going to be a great weekend. After it all, I had had my hotel reservations for two weeks. Anyway, I drove down by myself and met my buddies. We had a heck of an evening. The bands were jamming, and it got to be around 11:30 p.m., so I decided to head out to the hotel.

Well, I walked up to the reservation desk, and you guessed it, they gave up my room after I specifically told them I would be in at the midnight hour. (BURN!) They practically kicked me out of there, so I called my wife, and Darlene got on it. While I was driving around in no man's land, pretty hot and upset, I made it to a couple of places, but the landscape was not that good, if you get my drift.

Well, I told her I was going to sleep on top of a hill where there was a Walmart. I drove up, about to put my seat back and sleep in the parking lot, and Darlene called and said a hotel was holding a room for me. I was 30 miles away, but close to 3:00 in the morning, I finally made it. I was all stressed out and tired, but the Lord was with me. Believe it or not, I was even closer to the prison the next morning.

The visit with Gary went great and I stayed a few hours then headed back to Norman, OK. It was late Sunday afternoon when I made it home and I needed to get ready for my 11:00 a.m. Monday meeting with secret agent man. It was Monday morning, September16th, 2016. I drove over to the probation dept. and I sat there quietly waiting. About 10 minutes later, an officer came out to get me and we went to his office.

I sat and we started talking. To me, it was more of an interrogation. He started asking me questions about the ministry, and all of a sudden, he handed me this letter from an inmate that the prison had intercepted, and it was bad. He was asking me all kinds of questions about the murder, helping him get out, and bringing more drugs in the facility which to me was a big lie from the pits of hell.

I told agent man that I would like a copy of that letter and he told me that I could get a copy later. I was very adamant about getting a copy of that letter, but he said later. He would never give me a copy of it.

So as I was sitting there being interrogated, I asked him, "Do I need an attorney?"

He said, "If you want. You can leave whenever you want."

I said, "No, I have nothing to hide."

All of a sudden, he asked me why I go from Norman to McAlester to the Oklahoma State Pen, and it just came out of my mouth, I told him, "I am an Ambassador for Christ."

He just looked at me and then he asked me about my prescription list of what medicines I was on. I told him I had everything about me on paper, except the picture of the concrete mixer of the accident I was in. So, I pulled it out and he had a look on his face like, "Oh, so that's what happened!" God had me prepared.

He was still interrogating me, so I finally said, "Really, what else do you want to know?"

He told me, "Ya know, Mike, I think you have been pretty honest with me today."

Then he wrote this scale on a piece of paper from 1 through 100, and he made a mark on it. He said, "I think you are right here on telling me the truth," and he marked it at 97 %. He asked me, "Where are you?"

I marked mine at 98%. He looked at me and said, "I know you're lying. Where is that 2% you are not telling me about?"

I said I'm not lying, but there may be something else I just can't think of or remember."

I know this sounds crazy, but I should have marked the scale to 100%, but GOD was still in control.

All of a sudden, he pulls a pencil out of his desk drawer and he asked, "Do you know what this is?"

I said, "Yes, a pencil."

"Do you know what is at the end of this?" he asked.

I said, "Yes, an eraser."

He said in a smart voice, "You know you can easily take this pencil with an eraser and easily erase that 2% you're lying to me about."

I said, "There may be something, and if I find anything else, I will notify you."

I stood up and told him, "I'm out of here."

Isaiah 5:20-
*Woe unto them that call evil good, and good evil, that put darkness for light, and light for darkness, that put bitter for sweet, and sweet for bitter.*

I continued the next three months to go down to O.S.P. and nobody told me any different. I confronted the inmate that wrote that letter, and all he told me was that the man came to him also and asked him to write the letter and asked, "What do you have to lose, you're here for life."

I told him, "You see what you did to me and how the devil used you?" and he just shrugged his shoulders and said, "Oh well." He had a bad hernia and before I left, he let me pray for him.

It was January of 2017, and I was not scheduled for a visit. I called the chaplain and he told me I could come on down. I had a heaviness in my spirit to pray for an individual that was going to be executed. Even some of the guards were tripping, asking me, "What are you doing down here? It's not your day."

I handed them a letter from the chaplain for my special visit. I got down to H-block where they house the death row inmates. I made it down to pray for the inmate and visit a few others that I would usually see. They were very thankful for the visit. I stayed a few hours and headed home.

February came and Doc and I were the only ones to go that following 3rd Thursday of the month. We were sitting at McDonald's in McAlester eating breakfast and the phone call came that I was suspended. We looked at each other and said, "What the heck?"

We called the head chaplain of D.O.C., he told us that he would talk to us later. I had called his office number of times and they refused to meet with me or have an appeal process. He told one of my fellow preachers that if I could get something in writing stating that I was in good standing, he would see what he could do. Well, I got a letter from our local sheriff that I was in good standing and I sent him the letter that I was in good standing with Cleveland county jail.

The chaplain e-mailed me and gave me the class date to renew my badges, so I went and did the class in Oct. 2019. For 8 hours, I went through the training and received my badges the following week after our team member called the prison. I called D.O.C., and they told me they couldn't help me. I was still suspended.

So here I wait on the Lord patiently. I continue to do Cleveland County jail and the Juvenile Detention in OKC, but since the China virus (Covid-19) hit, things have been on delay mode. But the Lord has kept me busy with writing letters and sending out bibles and other Christian books, and still doing one-on-one visits behind the glass at Cleveland county.

The first few years, I was running hard for the Lord with this, walking in LOVE, and trying to reach the folks that are on death row and beyond. But if you think of it in a spiritual realm, I guess we are all on death row waiting for the day we meet our God.

I Corinthians 1:27-
*But God hath chosen the foolish things of this world to confound the wise, and God hath chosen the weak things of the world to confound the things which are mighty.*

Hebrews 9:27-
*And it is appointed unto men once to die, after this the judgment.*

2 Corinthians-
*We are confident, I say, and willing rather be absent from the body, and to be present with the Lord.*

Over the past few years, there have been over 3,000 souls that have surrendered their lives through Christ. It is all done by Faith, and the leading of the Holy Spirit. Believe me when I tell you my story, I never wanted this. I always enjoyed sin to the fullest, but God had other ideas, all because of my praying grandmother. Amen. My stepsons, Paul and Gary, are out of prison and living for the Lord, too. Their lives are testimonies in themselves.

On November 15th, 2015, my friend, Robby had tickets to see the Boston Celtics play the OKC Thunder at Oklahoma City, so he asked me if I wanted to go.

I said, "Sure!" We entered the Chesapeake Arena close to tip off time. It was a good game with a close score. All of a sudden, with about 6:39 to go in the game, there was a time out, so Robby went to the rest room.

Out of nowhere, things went in slow motion for me for about 20 seconds. I looked over at one of the referees and he was walking in slow motion. The fans in the stands to the left of me were clapping in slow motion, and this all happened in about 20 seconds.

The Lord told me, "LOOK AROUND, MIKE. THIS IS ALL GOING TO END SOON," then everything went back to normal. Robby came back and the Celtics went on a 15-0 run and won the game 100-85. Now fast forward 2020, it did all end because of the Covid-19 virus. It reminded me of the time in Branson, MO when the Lord talked to me through his spirit. Take it as you will, but the Scripture says:

*Numbers 23:19-* "God is not a man, that he should lie; neither the son of man, that he should repent: hath he said, and shall he not do it? or hath he spoken, and shall he not make it good?"

Romans 6:23 tells us-

*For the wages of sin is DEATH, but the GIFT of GOD is eternal LIFE through Jesus Christ our Lord.*

Well, this is my journey with the King. (It's ironic my old assistant pastors, Al and Ginger Boles, that was the name of their ministry. Al has been with the Lord for 5 years and Ginger is still praying, believing, and encouraging the Wayside, with her love and support.)

I just want you all to know that you're loved and encouraged every day, no matter what you have done in your life. God can use you!

John 10:10-
*The thief come not, but for to steal, and to kill,*
*and to destroy, I am come that they have life, and*
*that they might have it more abundantly.*

I could go on and on and I am sure this story will continue as I continue to battle the forces of good and evil, but good will always prevail. To me, if you're not being attacked in the spiritual realm as I have been, you're not doing the Lord's work, so just keep pressing on for the good and don't give up.

This was never to be a "religious trip," but as I call it, a relationship with the Lord. Because if I did it my way, it would have never worked, and I would have never made it this far without the leading of the Holy Spirit. God's grace endures forever. We are all going to die one day. What is your choice, smoking or non? There are no second chances.

LOVE, HOPE, FAITH, without LOVE nothing else matters, and for me, at times it is the hardest. You will, I will, and people will always try and do you harm, especially the ones closest to your heart. Amen. I LOVE You. Thanks for reading, And I hope this stirs up your faith in GOD.

No matter where you're at or what you have done, please say this prayer from your heart, and it is between you and God:

"Dear heavenly Father, I come to you in the name of Jesus to receive salvation. I believe Jesus is your Son, and that He died for my sins, and that you raised Him from the dead. I ask you to come into my heart and life and to forgive me of my sins. I confess you as Lord and accept the gift of salvation. In Jesus name, Amen."

If you just prayed that prayer, welcome to the family of GOD! Now remember, this is NOT a magic wand or a quick fix to all your problems, but it is a start. No matter what happens with your life keep doing this:

Philippians 3:14-
*I press toward the mark for the prize of the high
calling of GOD in CHRIST JESUS.*

# Acknowledgements

I would like to thank God, my Heavenly Father, and his Son, Jesus Christ, for saving my life over the years. I hope my story blesses everyone that picks up this book and reads it. And my prayer through hope and faith is that it touches everyone here, at home and abroad. All you have to say is, "JESUS!" if you forget anything after reading. Thanks, and GOD BLESS!

I would also like to thank my beautiful, precious wife, Darlene, who led me to the Lord back in 1990-1991. I am thankful for her loving me, protecting me, and putting up with me, especially during and after the accident. Darlene, you have walked with me through trials and tribulations, as the Lord said we would have them. Thank you also for letting this testimony be possible. My heart will always be grateful, and our bond of marriage will never be broken. Amen!

I would also like to thank Al and Ginger Boles for never giving up on me. My heart will always be thankful for your generosity with countless meals and Sunday football games, and your financial support in keeping the ministry going, and making this book a possibility.

I would also like to thank my immediate family, friends, and foes. May God Bless you all!

Matthew 6:9-15(KJV), After this manner, therefore pray ye, Our Father which art in Heaven Hallowed be thy name, thy kingdom come thy will be done in earth as it is in Heaven, Give us this day our daily bread. And forgive us our debts, as we forgive our debtors, and lead us not into temptation but deliver us from evil, for thine is the kingdom & power and the glory forever, forever AMEN.

The reason I close with the Lord's Prayer is because it was the one my mother made me learn growing up, and believe me, as I was learning or trying to learn the prayer, I would always watch "ALL IN THE FAMILY" through the kitchen and living room doorway. LOL!

I am very thankful because there are many times on my NOMAD journey that I needed it, and no matter how many evil predicaments I was in, I always prayed that prayer, and GOD listened and protected me.

So, this story & book is dedicated to my father Bernie Luciani and my mother Mary Luciani forever in my heart. Dad went to be with the Lord on May 10th, 2020 on Mother's Day. PEACE OUT! LOVE YOU ALL!

A special blessing to the publishers, Mark & Melissa Mingle. Without them, this would have not been possible. (And a special shout out for your patience. Love ya!)

*Cover image: Michael Luciani was called The Troll by his band members. The cover image is original art created based on his nickname.

WAYSIDE MINISTRIES
Michael & Darlene Luciani
PO Box 685
Norman, OK 73070
mikeswaysideministries@yahoo.com

9 780999 650738